From the Hearth
to the
Open Road

From the Hearth to the Open Road

A FEMINIST STUDY OF AGING IN CONTEMPORARY LITERATURE

Barbara Frey Waxman

CONTRIBUTIONS IN WOMEN'S STUDIES,
NUMBER 113

GREENWOOD PRESS
NEW YORK • WESTPORT, CONNECTICUT • LONDON

Library of Congress Cataloging-in-Publication Data

Waxman, Barbara Frey.
    From the hearth to the open road :   a feminist study of aging in
contemporary literature / Barbara Frey Waxman.
         p.   cm.—(Contributions in women's studies, ISSN 0147-104X ;
no. 113)
    Includes bibliographical references.
    ISBN 0-313-26650-6 (lib. bdg. : alk. paper)
    1. American fiction—Women authors—History and criticism.
    2. Canadian fiction—Women authors—History and criticism.
    3. English fiction—Women authors—History and criticism.
    4. Feminism and literature—History—20th century.   5. Women and
literature—History—20th century.   6. Aging in literature.
    I. Title. II. Series.
    PS374.F45W39   1990
    810'.9'9287—dc20   89-25701

British Library Cataloguing in Publication Data is available.

Library of Congress Catalog Card Number: 89-25701
ISBN: 0-313-26650-6
ISSN: 0147-104X

First published in 1990

Greenwood Press, 88 Post Road West, Westport, CT 06881
An imprint of Greenwood Publishing Group, Inc.

Printed in the United States of America

∞™

The paper used in this book complies with the
Permanent Paper Standard issued by the National
Information Standards Organization (Z39.48-1984).

10 9 8 7 6 5 4 3 2 1

To the memories of my mother, Florence Frey, and my grand-mothers, Eva Levine and Dora Frey, who first taught me about the possibilities of middle age and old age, and to my husband, Robert Waxman, whose encouragement made this study of the literature of aging possible and with whom I hope to share a spirited old age.

Contents

Acknowledgments

This study of the fiction of aging could not have been written without the help and advice of editors, colleagues, and friends. The librarians at the Randall Library of the University of North Carolina—Wilmington helped me with computer searches in the field of aging and literature and aided me in my research, from tracking down Canadian periodicals to finding turn-of-the-century magazines and recent reviews of Alice Adams's work; my thanks to Sue Cody, Louise Jackson, Ron Johnson, Debbie Sommer, and Joanna Wright. Fannie Peczenik, Carole Fink, and Bill Lowe helped me with the German language in my formulation of the term *Reifungsroman.* Sandra Eisdorfer read an early version of the entire manuscript, encouraged me to pursue it further, and made helpful suggestions for revisions. John Clifford, my colleague in the English department at the University of North Carolina—Wilmington, read an early version of the introduction and conclusion and gave me guidance on my use of literary theory in the manuscript. Sylvia Polgar, social work professor and colleague at the University of North Carolina—Wilmington, guided me toward major concepts and texts in gerontology. Eleanor Maxwell, sociologist and colleague at the University of North Carolina—Wilmington, read the introductory chapter, made helpful suggestions for revisions, and referred me to some important work being done on widows. Kathleen Berkeley, history professor and colleague at the University of North Carolina—Wilmington, read an early version of my chapter on Elizabeth Taylor and Barbara Pym and showed me how to tighten my style. All of these people, from their diverse disciplines, contributed their expertise and their humanity to this book, for which I am sincerely grateful.

I would also like to thank Marilyn Brownstein and the other readers of my manuscript at Greenwood Press for having faith in its potential to become a book. They have helped me to fulfill the promises made in the manuscript. Finally, I would like to thank my husband, Robert Waxman, whose encouragement, energy, and optimism helped me in innumerable ways to complete this project.

From the Hearth
to the
Open Road

Introduction: A New Fictional Genre—The *Reifungsroman*, or Fiction of Ripening

That Simone de Beauvoir, hailed by feminist theorist Toril Moi as "the greatest feminist theorist of our time" for her groundbreaking book on women's position in society, *The Second Sex* (92), also penned a pioneering philosophic, scientific, anthropological, and socially reformist work on aging and the elderly is an appropriate observation with which to begin this book. As a feminist committed to socialism, de Beauvoir joins other women and men " 'who are fighting to change women's condition, in association with the class struggle, but independently of it as well' " (Moi 92); the aim of social change is at the heart of her feminist theorizing. Change is also her purpose in *The Coming of Age* as she examines the fate of the elderly in Western society, declaring that "the meaning or the lack of meaning that old age takes on in any given society puts that whole society to the test, since it is this that reveals the meaning or the lack of meaning of the entirety of the life leading to that old age" (de Beauvoir 18). She condemns as "morally atrocious" the too-early and too-painful advent of old age countenanced by Western society. She is convinced older people need to be treated like people, not like material or machines, discarded when no longer sufficiently productive to society (805–6). And de Beauvoir envisions a utopian society in which the negative concept of old age would all but vanish because each individual would participate in communal life and "be an active, useful citizen at every age" (806). Having described the grim plight of the elderly, she rejects stopgap old-age policies and calls for radical change: "It is the whole system that is at issue and our claim cannot be otherwise than radical—change life itself" (807).

In the past three decades, increasing numbers of female fiction writers in the United States, Britain, and Canada have taken up de Beauvoir's dual challenges concerning women and the elderly. They have created a whole new genre of fiction that rejects negative cultural stereotypes of the old woman and aging, seeking to change the society that created these stereotypes. This new genre has been created by women writing about aging women for receptive readers in a rapidly aging society, just as its predecessor, the *Bildungsroman*, was widely read by a more youthful society. Like the *Bildungsroman*, this new genre displays unique characteristics of form, tone, narrative perspective, characterization, theme, plot, and imagery. I call this genre, in a feminist literary critic's act of naming, the *Reifungsroman*, or novel of ripening—, opposing its central tenet to the usual notion of deterioration in old age. The name is inspired by septuagenarian writer May Sarton's optimistic concept of "ripening toward death in a fruitful way."

The emergence of the *Reifungsroman* and the popular journalistic essays that paved the way for it, later echoing and reinforcing it, are the subjects of this book. The book's purpose is threefold: to introduce and discuss the characteristics of this new genre by analyzing magazine essays and fiction on aging and exploring their effects on readers; to assess the social impact this genre is making on American, British, and Canadian cultures; and finally, endorsing Frank Lentricchia's view of literary critics as social critics, to foster social change regarding old age. American, Canadian, and British culture's antipathy toward the aging woman's body and persona, as well as their assignment of the older woman to the lower echelons of the second sex, must be changed. Like the *Reifungsromane* discussed here, this book seeks to break down Western culture's binary opposition between youth and age, with all positive attributions on the side of youth, and instead to create positive associations with age and even a new space where age is no longer an element of identity: an ageless utopia.

Before describing the characteristics of the *Reifungsroman* and exploring why this book concentrates on *Reifungsromane* about older women's experiences, as distinct from those of older men, we need to consider the social factors that have encouraged this proliferation of texts about aging, making public a subject heretofore almost as taboo as death in this century and sex in the preceding century. As Edward Said says, all texts are "worldly, to some degree they are events, . . . they are . . . a part of the social world, human life, and . . . the historical moments in which they are located and interpreted" (4). One social factor prompting texts about aging is the rapidly increasing population of older citizens in the United States, Britain, and Canada. The number of American citizens 65 and older has more than doubled since 1950, numbering about 28 million in 1986. The number of Americans over age 85 has more than quadrupled since 1950 to about 2.6 million. By the twenty-first century, as the baby boom generation enters "young old age" (ages 60–75), these numbers will swell enormously. Sociologists Alan Pifer and Lydia Bronte conservatively predict that by the year 2035, one-fifth to one-quarter of all Americans will be 65 or older. This situation will be accompanied by a decline in the number of children under age 16 (Pifer and Bronte 4). Moreover, all the other developed nations of the world are aging like the United States; many in Western Europe are even "older" than we are (Pifer and Bronte 5). What kinds of effects are these increasing numbers of elders having on the nations in which they live?

One effect is the visibility of activist elders in the political arena; they have considerable political clout and lobby successfully with government leaders. As sociologist Alice S. Rossi observes, "the needs of the elderly have become increasingly prominent in electoral campaigns and lobbying efforts on Congress, given their growing numbers, their much higher turnout in elections, and the rapid growth of voluntary associations and lobbies that represent their interests" (128). Among these voluntary organizations is the American Association of Retired Persons (AARP), with 28 million members, a staff of 1,200, and annual revenues of almost $200 million ("Old But Far"). When the AARP argues for federal financing of long-term medical care for the elderly, political candidates cannot afford not to listen, being aware of the percentages of older Americans who vote: in 1980, for example, 71% of Americans 55–64 voted, while only 36% of Americans 18–20 did, and overall only 55% of the country votes in presidential election years ("Old But Far"). As lobbyists, in addition, the AARP's people are rated highly "partly because they are unusually well informed . . . and partly because their approach is unflamboyant" ("Old But Far").

Perhaps a bit more flamboyant and eliciting more media coverage are the Gray Panthers, founded by Maggie Kuhn. The Gray Panthers bills itself as intergenerational in its membership and interests, working for the future welfare of all. But Maggie Kuhn also argues eloquently for "grass-roots Gray Power" and for political consciousness raising of the old to inspire political unity: "The self-determination which we seek cannot be achieved unless the people affected by decisions are involved in making, enforcing and monitoring them. . . . If we can open up new life styles that enable us to function with power and authority and influence, then we are working for the survival of society as a whole" (224–25). Kuhn asks elders to rethink the economic structures that prevent them from continuing to work, suggests that they try more communal living, and encourages residents of retirement villages and old age homes to become involved as voting members of these institutions, making policy and monitoring the performance of staff (225–26). Not coincidentally, Kuhn also labels herself a feminist and in her speeches frequently addresses the interlocking oppressions of sexism and ageism. Passivity and apathy are outworn notions of old age to this activist, and her dramatic visibility has surely inspired other elders, including those among the 50,000 who are members of the Gray Panthers, to reject the stereotype of old age as Golden Pond retirement. Together they have built a vital organization with an annual budget of half a million dollars.

Other political organizations also unite and represent the old, such as the National Council of Senior Citizens, with its labor union constituency of three million, the National Alliance of Senior

Citizens, the Senior Political Action Committee, the Older Women's League, and the Leadership Council of Aging Organizations. These organizations prepare media campaigns, legislative alerts, and political forums for their members. They also lobby successfully, having helped to abolish mandatory retirement age, to defeat cuts in social security benefits, to legalize generic drugs (Peirce and Choharis 1560–61), and to make age discrimination in employment illegal. Neal Peirce and Peter Choharis, writing for the *National Journal*, suggest that these groups succeed because they "are able to tap the time and skills of members who formerly held powerful positions in government or business" (1561).

The activist, even militant, stance of these elders serves not only to advance the political and economic needs of the old, but also to challenge the stereotype that old people are frail, dim-witted, and vegetating in nursing homes; in fact, only 5% of the elderly in the United States were institutionalized in 1980, and while the percentage for those over age 85 is greater (22%), many stay only briefly in nursing homes, recuperating or receiving terminal care (Siegel and Taeuber 101). Elders' political action groups, then, are educating younger Americans not to see old age as synonymous with ill health, dependency, and institutionalization. Sociologists Bernice and Dail Neugarten point out that because of elders' active life-styles, the line between middle age and old age is no longer clear; many retirees have their health, financial independence, and the energy to be involved in the lives of their children, politics, and community affairs, so that "age has become a poor predictor ... of a person's health, work status, family status, and therefore, also, of a person's interests, preoccupations, and needs" (35–36). The young old are leading fully robust, meaningful lives.

Despite these reports of vigor among the elderly, nevertheless, health care systems have felt the impact of the increasing elderly population in the United States, Britain, and Canada. And this impact inevitably has affected public opinion toward the elderly. The United States, with its mix of public programs, private insurance, and direct patient payment, has, as health policy and management expert Karen Davis observes, considerably more difficulty than Britain and Canada in controlling the level of resources devoted to health care for each segment of the population. The average annual cost of health care for a person aged 65 and over is much greater ($3,140 in 1981) than for those under 65 ($828). Most of these costs are underwritten by the federal government through Medicare and Medicaid. Davis predicts, however, that as the elderly population expands, the total health care expenses for the aged will increase from about $50 billion in 1978 to nearly $200 billion in the year 2000 (308).

With these financial demands comes some resentment from younger segments of the American people who see the elderly as a potential threat to "the welfare of younger generations and of society as a whole" (Callahan 320). Some younger people fear they will not get their fair share of health care benefits (Callahan 330). They are also unwilling to shoulder most of the financial burden for elders' and their own medical bills. Even those in Britain and Canada protected by complete government-financed medical care are not exempt from financial worries about elders' health care: on August 7, 1988, a front-page article by Steve Lohr in the *Sunday New York Times* disclosed the crisis in funding of Britain's National Health Service, with resulting shortages of medical staff and delays in surgical service; Lohr observed that "many of the problems confronting the service . . . are difficulties shared by the health systems of most developed nations, particularly the soaring costs of high-technology medicine and an aging population" (sec. 1, 1). These concerns draw battle lines between young and old.

Proposals have been made to meet these financial crises, such as distributing the costs of elders' health care among the whole population, or rationing health care for elders on the basis of ability to pay (Davis 300). Britain is also discouraging use of costly technologies for elderly patients (Avorn 293). However, this practice, biomedical ethicist Daniel Callahan points out, raises ethical issues about who should and should not get medical care. If we consider the "quality of life" factor in making the decision to treat or withhold treatment, the decision will normally "favor those age groups whose potentiality for an extended quality of life is greatest (self-evidently the young)," which could mean society's abandon-ment of the old (Callahan 332). Ageism, or prejudice toward the elderly, even among health care professionals, often underlies this medical decision making. When people debate health care issues for the old, they seem to overemphasize the ill health of the old. Davis, well educated on the issues, nevertheless uses dehumaniz-ing language that exaggerates the numbers of "the functionally impaired elderly" (315), people "with chronic illness or limited functional ability" (307). And Callahan focuses on the dying elderly, especially those "who end their days incompetent, incon-tinent, and grossly incapacitated, more dead than alive" (320). Jerome L. Avorn, M.D., explains the prejudice of American med-ical students and doctors toward care for the old as stemming from their having been trained to think that there is one cause of any illness, which they can cure; consequently, they feel "frustrated and even appalled by the realities [multiple causes of complexly related ailments] of geriatric practice" (Avorn 290–92). It is no wonder, then, that in 1985 there were fewer than a hundred geriatric physicians in the entire United States (Hill 1D). Clearly, medical training needs to include more study of age-related health needs to equip future doctors, regardless of specialization, to serve an aging population. And all health-care providers must study the ethical issues in medical care for elders.

Thus the social reality out of which this new literary discourse of aging comes is increasingly aware of and receptive toward the needs and interests of older people, but is still haunted by old negative stereotypes of senescence and is also troubled by new fears of the increasing numbers and escalating demands of elders. Recent scholarship by feminist theorists can address this disturbing dichotomy between youth and age still rife in Anglo-American culture, encouraging rethinking of the experience of aging, which has been especially burdensome for women. Such rethinking of a culture from a gendered viewpoint Myra Jehlen identifies as feminist: "Feminist thinking is really *re* thinking, an examination of the way certain assumptions about women and the female character enter into the fundamental assumptions that organize all our thinking" (189). One divisive assumption of American culture worth interrogating is that old age is, in May Sarton's words, a "foreign country" that youth, particularly the young woman, knows nothing about, has nothing in common with, fears, and xenophobically avoids. Hence age adds to the burden of women's oppression in a culture that still valorizes youthful beauty as a major source of a woman's power. Gender and age together are an example of what Paula A. Treichler calls "interlocking oppressions," which feminist theory is committed to examine in order to envision "possible futures" (Treichler 59). Feminist theory can examine older women's dual oppressions in order to eliminate them and move society toward a utopian future without the stigma of old age—de Beauvoir's ageless society.

Treichler makes another point: that feminist theory seeks the sources of the concept of gender and the dichotomization of the sexes, ultimately to reject this dichotomizing "in favor of the possibility of genetic, physiological, and psychological continuums" (61). Her point may be borrowed to conceptualize youth and age as an undemarcated continuum. This concept of a continuum could change the traditional roles assigned elders in our society as radically as the dissolving of gender polarities would prompt "a rethinking of . . . mothering, of our relations to others in the world, and of the family" (Treichler 61). Josephine Donovan similarly argues in *The New Feminist Moral Vision* that American culture's thinking needs to move "beyond the artificial and destructive divisions of masculine epistemology" (182). Although elders are now protected legally from age discrimination, socially the artificial divisions between youth and age still exist, with patriarchal culture assigning identity and social value to individuals on the basis of age and elders being devalued. Adopting a continuum could lessen this devaluation.

Like Donovan, feminist philosopher Jean Bethke Elshtain advocates a dismantling of patriarchal power-constructs and bipolar thinking through a feminist language that "bursts the bonds of social control and unexpectedly offers intimations of a life still-in-becoming" (142). Elshtain's thinking is useful in interrogating societal attitudes toward aging and treatment of the old, as she argues that we must articulate "a philosophy of mind that repudiates the old dualism . . . in favor of an account that unites mind and body, reason and passion, into a compelling account of human subjectivity and identity" (142). Repudiation of the dualism between youth and age—including youth's assignment of "Otherness" to the old—and increased recognition of the chronological spectrum of rich individuality are lessons from Elshtain's feminist theorizing that can help to expose and remedy negative attitudes toward aging.

Finally, Julia Kristeva in her essay "Women's Time" raises issues about gender that may be applied to age. She radically questions the whole notion of identity based on gender by positing a new "generation or signifying space" where the rivalry between maleness and femaleness becomes purely metaphysical; "difference" disintegrates in its nucleus (52). Kristeva's philosophical notion of gender can extend to age, encouraging society to neutralize the tension between youth and old age, a tension both within the individual who will experience these poles of life and between the young and the elderly. Kristeva's interrogation of gender also encourages us to question the use of chronological age as a basis for identity.

Thus feminist theorists' ideas about gender in society foster new thinking about aging in society. And there is little doubt that their ideas have joined with the social reality of aging populations to encourage the involvement of magazine journalists with the issues, themes, and language of aging. When aging becomes the focus of large numbers of magazine articles—"legitimate" examples of literature in their own right, as Terry Eagleton argues (1–16)—an ethos is created in which contemporary fiction writers can bring forth, for an increasingly receptive readership, a new literary genre that further dismantles patriarchal dualisms: the *Reifungsroman* or "novel of ripening."

A survey of journalistic essays on aging in the first chapter of this book, from the turn of the century to the present in the United

States, Britain, and Canada, shows how far these nations have moved toward associating energy, productivity, and integrity with senescence. The earliest essays on aging created some of the negative images, archetypes, and themes that later journalism and fiction on aging have had to dispel. The turn-of-the-century magazine essays' narrative points of view are often introspective, brooding, self-critical, even despondent about aging. The archetype of old age as hearthside retirement, indoor passivity, and deterioration appears, as does a mirror-gazing motif, in which the mirror reports old age's ravages, connecting senescence with repellent images of old hags and crones. For example, in an article titled "Being Happy in Old Age," which appeared in *Ladies' Home Journal* in March, 1900, Mrs. Burton Kingsland admonished her female readership to enjoy the "winter of life" and keep their hearts warmed, despite the bad news in the mirror, by clinging to family and loved ones: "we must hug the closer the joys of the fireside"; and she further advised, "If our looking-glasses tell us unpalatable truths we may always see ourselves at our best in the mirrors of loving and friendly eyes" (10). This narrow, unexciting, though warm, secure, and clearly sentimentalized haven of family was what a woman supposedly could look forward to in her old age. The visage of the old hag or crone, with gray hair, wrinkled skin, age spots, and sagging facial muscles—a nightmare to women in a culture where their appearance was of great importance—would make a woman repugnant to anyone but her family, suggests Mrs. Kingsland. So at a time when a woman might begin to feel liberated from the claustrophobic indoor life of a wife and mother, the onerous duties of managing a household and raising children to adulthood, at a time when the outdoor world and adventure might finally be beckoning to her, the message is that this repugnant old woman must stay home, keep the family ties, and not risk repelling other people or being rejected by them. Keeping women sheltered to the last is Mrs. Kingsland's point.

Mrs. Kingsland's essay is not atypical for 1900 in America. And many negative images of old age's ravages still exist. A glance at any birthday card rack will show that ageism continues to haunt

American culture; stereotyped, crass remarks about physical deterioration, the inability to perform sexually, the inability to do anything but sit in a rocking chair and rock, parade as contemporary humor in many birthday cards today. Essays about aging in such magazines as *Vogue* and *McCall's* at times give a similarly negative message, showing their authors' prejudices against aging by offering remedies for age spots and sagging muscles, antidotes for gray hair, and camouflages for increasingly shapeless bodies.

However, there is some cause for optimism about the treatment of aging women in recent popular journalism. Images of "the open road" sometimes replace the hearthside, suggesting that old age for women is becoming a time of discovery, liberation, and adventure, offering women an opportunity to form new ties, not just to reinforce old ones. The introspective narrative structure and the mirror-gazing imagery of articles on aging become more celebratory. Some outmoded attitudes and norms about appearance and conduct for older women are rejected. Even conventional magazines like *McCall's*, *Saturday Evening Post*, and *Newsweek* reflect these changing attitudes. Margery Finn Brown, an elder, declares in a June 1982 *McCall's*, "I like myself more, I am myself in old age as I was not, as I could never have been in youth or middle age" (66). New commitments, self-discovery, and a joyful self-affirmation in old age are the new themes of aging. The energetic, prolific romance writer Barbara Cartland, for example, in a January–February 1985 *Saturday Evening Post* article, ridicules the old-fashioned hearthside archetype, denying that " 'Granny likes to sit by the fire knitting' or 'old people need peace and quiet' " (63). Her position is corroborated by biographical sketches of "salty old women" in *Ms.* And in a *Newsweek* feature article dated November 1, 1982, "Growing Old, Feeling Young," geriatric specialist Dr. George Pollack reminds Americans that the elderly "are people who continue to have hopes, dreams, desires . . . and who want still to be useful to the people around them" (Gelman 60).

These declarations in magazine writing of the 1970's and 1980's that the old are productive and have passions, verve, and a sense of futurity, just like the young, weaken the traditional polarities between age and youth and also create a receptive readership for more complex fictions of aging. The authors of these new fictions of aging feel a similar urgency to humanize the elderly and link old age with productivity and futurity.

Most *Reifungsromane* are written by women. Why? Perhaps aging is of more interest to women writers and readers because elderly women outnumber elderly men three to two: most elderly over age 75 are female (Siegel and Taeuber 85–86). Or perhaps it is because older women have been greater victims of ageism in a sexist and youth-oriented culture, fueling the anger of women writers. On the other hand, aging women writers, active and ripening themselves, may reflect themselves as they celebrate aging women in their fiction. The Women's Movement has also encouraged feminist thinking since the 1950's about all the stages of a woman's life cycle. This is not to say that male fiction writers have not shown interest in aging and contributed to this new genre; John Gardner's *October Light* and I. B. Singer's *Old Love* come to mind. But recent feminist research across disciplines suggests that male writers' characterizations of the "ages of man" in male *Reifungsromane* are likely to be very different from women writers' presentations of the "ages of women" in female *Reifungsromane*; women's lives do not completely conform to male paradigms of experience and development observed by male researchers and thus need to be examined separately from men's lives.

For example, sociologist Nancy Chodorow, in her important book *The Reproduction of Mothering*, examines gender distinctions in interactions between mother and child. She shows how identification between mother and daughter and the contrasting development of difference between mother and son result in earlier separation of son from mother and sustained symbiosis between daughter and mother well into adolescence; consequently, the daughter's ego boundaries are not as firmly established as the son's: "Because of their mothering by women, girls come to experience themselves as less separate than boys, as having more permeable ego boundaries. Girls come to define themselves more in relation to others" (93). Psychologist Lucy Rose Fischer extends this timetable of mother-daughter attachment even further, offering evidence that daughters till about age 40 keep "some sense of child position in their relationships with their mothers" (9).

And psychologist Carol Gilligan, in her groundbreaking study of women's development, *In a Different Voice*, extends into adulthood Chodorow's ideas about gender's role in relationships, individuation, and identity. She gives convincing evidence that women associate identity with intimacy (13) and emphasize attachment as important throughout the human life cycle (23). Moreover, women not only define themselves through their relationships, but also judge their own maturity "in terms of their ability to care" (Gilligan 17). This is in stark contrast to the male model of development touted by male psychologists, which equates maturity with "individual achievement . . . and . . . personal autonomy" (Gilligan 17).

Gilligan's effort to break "the silence of women in the narrative of adult development" (156) also corroborates the need for studies of aging women, as distinct from aging men: "women not only reach mid-life with a psychological history different from men's and face at that time a different social reality having different possibilities for love and for work, but they also make a different sense of experience, based on their knowledge of human relationships" (Gilligan 172). Pauline Bart, in her study of depression in middle-aged women, furthers this notion of gender differences in life-stage experiences, noting that middle age is traditionally in American society the "empty nest" stage for women, an end to her mothering role, "the role that had given her life meaning, the only role she considered important for her" (Bart 130). The woman overcommitted to the maternal role feels worthless, useless, and depressed in middle age: "If one's sense of worth comes from other people [one's children] rather than from one's own accomplishments, it follows that when such people depart, one is left with an empty shell in place of a self" (Bart 138). Men, in contrast, are often at the peak of their careers in middle age; so when their children leave home, they do not experience the same feelings of worthlessness as their female peers. Gerontologist Phyllis Silverman also notes gender differences in her studies of widows. While widows thrive alone, widowers do *not* fare very well. One simply cannot generalize about human middle age and senescence from male—or female—experiences of aging.

Other feminists have attempted to readjust the English language to reflect these differences between female and male experience through the life cycle. Dale Spender, for example, constructs a new kind of general index for her book *Women of Ideas and What Men Have Done to Them*, claiming that women have different "ways of classifying and analyzing the world" (787); consequently, her index is an effort "to conceptualise the categories as they relate to women—even though this has necessitated the coinage of new terms" (Spender 791). Spender's sensitivity to the differences between male and female aging in a patriarchal society is also apparent: "whereas the worth of a man may increase with age in a society ordered by men (so that life merely begins at forty) that of a woman decreases with age (so that life ends at thirty . . .), with the result that, while society may sit at the feet of elderly male gurus, women almost never experience such veneration" (639). Similarly, in their *Feminist Dictionary*, Cheris Kramarae and Paula A. Treichler recast in feminist terms male conceptions of female experience prevalent in male lexicographic traditions (12). Their entries on age, ageism, aging, and old age are especially instructive. These entries point out that women suffer more from ageism than men because of a double standard of aging; they counter it by emphasizing self-actualization in old age, the opportunity to "grow toward the light"; they also reenvision old women as wise "in spiritual knowledge" and thus "a threat to male dominance" (Kramarae and Treichler 38–39; 313).

Feminist literary critics have also shown that female accounts of life-cycle experiences recorded in fiction differ markedly from male accounts. Elizabeth Abel, Marianne Hirsch, and Elizabeth Langland, in their study of female versions of the *Bildungsroman*, assert that "the sex of the protagonist modifies every aspect of a particular *Bildungsroman*: its narrative structure, its implied psychology, its representation of social pressures" (5). Narratives about young women growing up extend the definition of the *Bildungsroman* because "while male protagonists struggle to find a hospitable context in which to realize their aspirations, female protagonists must frequently struggle to voice any aspirations whatsoever. . . . Social options are often so narrow that they preclude explorations of her milieu" (Abel 6–7). Unlike the heroes of *Bildungsromane*, who enter the world, learn its rules, and embrace adulthood in youth, female protagonists excluded from a public life are confined to the inner life and ordinarily undergo a deferred maturation or awakening later in life after they experience the inadequacies of marriage and motherhood (Abel 7–8; 12).

Like Abel, Hirsch, and Langland, then, I am concerned with female versions of experience, analyzing how gender and other cultural factors shape a genre that extends the *Bildungsroman* into middle and old age. Also like them, I describe the distinctive features of a genre, the female *Reifungsroman*. In doing so, I pay tribute to the women writers who, interpreting the social and psychological experience of aging by the female body and mind, move beyond patriarchal paradigms of human development; they perform an invaluable service, as Dale Spender notes: "Being able to generate, validate and control our own knowledge about ourselves and society is . . . of critical importance to women, for we have been 'victims' insofar as we have been dependent on males for public knowledge of ourselves" (369). Finally, I assess the cultural work being accomplished by this genre, how it may be changing the attitudes of readers toward the elderly in the United States, Britain, and Canada.

The women writers represented here are of established or clearly growing literary reputation who have published a recognized body of fiction. Many works on the aging experience by less well known authors, such as *Union Street*, by Pat Barker, *They*, by Marya Mannes, or *Waking*, by Eva Figes, could have been included here. But I have limited my sample to more prominent and already influential writers as they contribute acknowledged political power and influence to the discourse of aging.

What, then, are the characteristics of female fictions of aging, or *Reifungsromane*? *Reifungsromane* are frequently confessional in tone and structure. They are also usually characterized by great mobility, recursiveness, or rambling in narrative structure, and passion as well as candor in the disclosures of the protagonists, perhaps because their authors endeavor, like many younger feminist writers, "to nourish our societies with a more flexible and free discourse, one able to name what has thus far never been an object of circulation in the community: the enigmas of the body, the dreams, secret joys, shames, hatreds of the second sex" (Kristeva 50). The "male" power of naming, accorded to men since Adam, is claimed by these authors, whose narrators defiantly "name" the old woman, her passions, longings, joys, resentments, bodily and emotional hungers, and achievement of integrity.

The stories and novels of aging discussed in the chapters that follow depict women's rite of passage into senescence thematically as a ripening process. In addition to portraying this ripening, these works also record changes in the protagonists, especially their embrace of new commitments and interests. While *Reifungsromane* do not paint a uniformly rosy picture of old age—they include themes of physical and psychic pain; loneliness; alienation from family and youthful society; self-doubt; feelings of uselessness; and grief over the loss of friends, mental acuity, and physical energy—there is, nevertheless, an opening up of life for many of these aging heroines as they literally take to the open road in search of themselves and new roles in life. The narrative structure for these works, then, is commonly a journey, frequently a meandering one, in quest of self-knowledge, self-development, and a role for the future. The narrative point of view is usually first-person, accompanied by a stream-of-consciousness method, or third-person limited omniscient, confined to the elder in a youthful world. Both viewpoints enable readers to identify closely with the aging self in motion. For example, Kate Brown in Doris Lessing's *The*

Summer Before the Dark and Avey Johnson in Paule Marshall's *Praisesong for the Widow* physically and psychically journey toward more fully realized selves and life still-in-becoming. Kate leaves her suburban London home and moves through London, Turkey, and Spain while Avey leaves middle-class North White Plains, New York, for the Caribbean. Both return stronger, more integrated, and truer to themselves. As Annis Pratt explains in *Archetypal Patterns in Women's Fiction*, the traditional *Bildungsroman* with a female protagonist depicts a character who does not travel outside the domestic enclosure and who grows "down," not up: self-development is thwarted as the female protagonist conforms to the restrictive cultural milieu of female adulthood (15). In contrast, the women in *Reifungsromane* develop and expand more as they grow old than they did as they grew up—or perhaps they truly grow up at last.

Whether or not they are literally traveling, these protagonists usually make an internal journey to their past through dreams and frequent flashbacks, essential features of the *Reifungsroman* narrative structure. As they travel, they gradually come to terms with crucial decisions they made as youths; with past experiences, often sexual, that influenced their lives; and with their cultural roots. Then they try to chart a new course either into or through old age, which they embark on at the end of the work. Usually they have become revitalized, newly self-knowledgeable, self-confident, and independent before they move forward. If the protagonist of the *Reifungsroman* dies at the end of the story, it is commonly after she has grown in a significant way.

Thus intimate narrations, realistic characterizations, strongly evocative descriptions of the mental and physical baggage carried by the old, and interior views of their treatment by younger characters all blur the boundaries between young and old, reality and fantasy, belonging and Otherness, integrity and fragmentation, rationality and senility. These *Reifungsromane* insistently draw readers into the world of senescence, enabling them to identify with the heroines, to experience elders' passions, joys, and hopes, often mingled with a frustrating sense of helplessness. Readers come to think as elders do about the hostile society around them, about health, about dependency, and about dying. These works give readers experiences with older human beings in a way that gerontologists and psychologists cannot. Clinical specialists observe, analyze, draw conclusions, and prescribe remedies sometimes, but a clinical case history of an elderly woman, by its very nature, does not allow a reader briefly to become elderly at the age of 30, to assume the body and mind of an 80 year old. Immersing oneself in the visceral prose of this genre, a young reader may, as Louise Rosenblatt suggests, be able to identify with octogenarians, "to enter into their behavior and their emotions" (40). Readers may also be dizzied by the innovative, mobile quality of the writing, a quality that Helene Cixous in her essay "The Laugh of the Medusa" characterizes as the essence of woman writing: "flying in language and making it fly, . . . jumbling the order of space . . . emptying structures, and turning propriety upside down" (887). *Reifungsromane* have this kind of disorienting and radicalizing effect on readers, temporarily transforming their identities, dissolving barriers between real and imagined, remembered and experienced, young and old, and hence disburdening readers of many negative expectations about old age and the Otherness of elders.

Such identification has fruitful psychological and social consequences. Younger readers may acknowledge elders as part of the human community while also acquiring greater understanding of and preparation for their own passage into middle age and senescence. Older readers may gain a fuller perspective on what they are experiencing, as well as reaffirmation of their humanity. Both attitudinal changes challenge the ageism that young and old often feel. As gerontologist Robert Butler points out, "Ageism allows the younger generations to see older people as different from themselves; thus they subtly cease to identify with their elders as human beings," the ultimate consequence of which is self-hatred when they themselves become elders ("Older, Stronger, Wiser" 10). Thus ageism is a double-edged sword attacking the vitality of young and old alike. Fictional texts and the literary critical responses to these texts emerge as new social events that resist this ageism and challenge the authority of youth (Said 4–5). These texts foster what Frank Lentricchia urges writers and critics to foster: "a collective will for change" (37) in societies where change in conception and treatment of aging is overdue.

The general themes of ripening and expansion of the self in the *Reifungsroman* take particular forms relevant to each stage of life, from middle age (ages 40–60) to young old age (healthy people aged 60–84) to frail old age (usually over age 85, but may include younger people suffering ill health). Thus, after an initial chapter on popular journalism and aging, this book is divided chronologically and thematically into three sections, according to protagonists' ages and the themes that reflect their place on the age continuum.

Chapter 2 deals with fiction that depicts the middle-aged woman's reacquaintance with her past self and redefining of a new, truer self. In this fiction, middle-aged women confront the loss of sex appeal, the diminution of energy, "empty nest" emotions, adjustments to widowhood, and the burden of elderly parent care. Also apparent are the joys of the middle-aged woman, her new independence, increasing ability to express herself, and courage to try new roles. In Chapter 2, Doris Lessing's *The Summer Before the Dark* and *The Diaries of Jane Somers* are discussed in relation to three stories, miniature *Reifungsromane*, from Alice Adams's collection, *To See You Again*. Doris Lessing, a writer of international repute, is best known for her novel *The Golden Notebook*, and Adams, a San Franciscan, enjoys a growing reputation in the United States, her recent novel *Second Chances*, also about the "no longer young," having received the approbation of many American critics. The solitary summer odyssey of Lessing's Kate Brown, her self-discoveries and graceful acceptance of her graying self in many ways parallel the changes in Adams's three heroines as they acquire the skills to live alone and age mellowly, "like a weathering country house." Lessing's *The Diaries of Jane Somers* depicts new love in late middle age as well as parent care and the problems of a growing class of women whom gerontologist Elaine Brody calls "the women in the middle." This chapter, like chapters 2 and 3, includes works that portray both American culture and either British or Canadian culture because instructive differences emerge, corroborating de Beauvoir's claim that "the meaning or the lack of meaning that old age takes on in any given society puts that whole society to the test" (18).

Chapter 3 focuses on three works that belie the notion that young old age is a mere winding down from life's emotional and physical commitments into a Golden Pond tranquility, precursor to death. In Elizabeth Taylor's *Mrs. Palfrey at the Claremont*, Barbara Pym's *Quartet in Autumn*, and Paule Marshall's *Praisesong for the Widow*, the four protagonists, spinsters and widows, become in their 60's and 70's more passionate and more committed, to other individuals, to their own ethnic culture, and to the excitement of life's possibilities. While death may hover in the background of Pym's and Taylor's novels, love and sexual feeling are startlingly evident in the foreground. Love is also evident in Marshall's novel, the protagonist's rekindled love for family and her ancestral roots in the Caribbean and Africa. This chapter compares the British to the African American aging experience for women. The increasingly turbulent, increasingly rich and vital lives of these novels' heroines help lay to rest the stereotypical equating of senescence with a cocoonlike, dozing passivity.

Even when faced with the debilitating effects of old age and illness that force a dependency on others, the frail elderly do not and need not succumb to mental passivity. Chapter 3 focuses on this issue of dependency and the strong emotions related to it in two elderly heroines, Caroline Spencer of May Sarton's *As We Are Now* and Hagar Shipley of Margaret Laurence's *The Stone Angel*. Sarton is a prolific American poet, diarist, and fiction writer, a paradigm of the energetic elder, still producing and writing about aging in her 70's despite bouts with major illness. In *As We Are Now*, she writes of 76-year-old Caro's incapacitation by a heart attack. Laurence, sadly neglected by American critics although preeminent among Canadian authors, provides an early prototype of the truly aged heroine in 90-year-old Hagar (*The Stone Angel* was published in 1964 while the other works in this book appeared in the 1970's and 1980's). The two heroines challenge dependency with an intense anger that scorches readers. These characters are angry at their failing bodies and minds and furious at the families, nursing homes, and hospital personnel on whom they must rely. Yet both women move beyond anger into philosophy. They order their lives by reassessing their pasts, coming to terms with where they have been and who they are, and then determining where they are headed. Readers reminisce with them, fume with them, ache with them, and expand with them as they experience new love, intoxicating freedom, and revitalized self-pride. The *Reifungsroman* is not depressing.

The concluding chapter summarizes the literary innovations of the *Reifungsroman* and the aging experiences conveyed in this genre, reconsidering how the authors of these works write the aging woman's body and mind in ways that encourage positive attitudinal changes in society. I also consider how the *Reifungsroman*, while instructing readers about interactions between aged parents and their relatives and friends, moves us all closer to that ageless society. In short, my concerns in this last chapter are aesthetic, philosophical, humanitarian, utopian: the concerns of the feminist literary critic committed to fostering "a collective will for change" in the treatment of the aging woman and in societal attitudes toward senescence.

1

Popular Journalism's Treatment of Old Age and the Aging Experience

That the average human being is concerned about the "foreign country" of old age and the journey to it is evident from even a cursory glance at a periodicals index like *Readers' Guide to Periodical Literature* or *Poole's Index*. Checking from as far back as 1890 up to 1920, and then perusing indexes of the 1950's through 1980's, I discovered that there were always a substantial number of articles in popular magazines on growing old and being old. True, many of these articles dutifully reinforce the traditional binary opposition between youth and age, perpetuating myths about old age, such as the calm serenity of the "twilight" years; the threat of physical deterioration and mental dotage; the desirability of a cozy place by the family's fireside to curl up and knit; the inevitability of the female's transformation into the ugly old hag and recipes for slowing that transformation. Yet a fair number, especially in the 1970's and 1980's, strive to explode myths and stereotypes of aging, to educate the public about the pervasiveness of ageism, and to depict age not in opposition to, but on a continuum with youth.

Whether these articles are negative or positive or, more commonly, ambivalent in their portrayals of the elderly, however, they demonstrate the public's strong interest in the subject, if popular magazines such as *Time*, *McCall's*, *Saturday Evening Post*, *Maclean's* (Canada's weekly newsmagazine), or *Ladies' Home*

Journal have their finger on the pulse of the public, as they and their sales figures claim. These magazines have helped to create a climate in which a serious fiction on aging might flourish.

The sampling of old magazine articles from 1890 to 1920, from the American magazines *Woman's Home Companion, Ladies' Home Journal, Littell's Living Age, Harper's Bazaar, Atlantic Monthly,* and *The Nation,* as well as the British magazines *Fortnightly Review, The Cornhill Magazine, Chamber's Edinburgh Journal,* and *The Spectator,* depicts youth as triumphant antagonist to age. These articles, patently moral in tone, also try to give advice on how to reach old age—through temperance and virtuous conduct—and on how to act properly when one arrives there; proper conduct for elders is vastly different from proper conduct for youth. Moreover, some of the articles treat old women more negatively than old men, especially on the issue of physical appearance. They reinforce the old adage quoted in a January, 1904 *Woman's Home Companion* article called "The Flying Years": "A woman is as old as she looks, a man as old as he feels" (Vance 17). Finally, because in the period of 1890 to 1920 old age and youth were more strictly construed as a binary opposition, the pleasures of old age that these articles describe are tamer and less varied than the pleasures of elders detailed in 1970's and 1980's articles. The earlier articles associate old age with the end of productivity and a decreased vitality—including sexual vitality.

Mrs. Burton Kingsland first warns us of the physical negatives of aging for women and then shows us how to take heart when old age assails us. The tone of her article is both alarmist and exhortatory. "Being Happy in Old Age," which appeared in the March 1900 issue of *Ladies' Home Journal,* uses images central to the literature of aging: the hearthside and the mirror. These images help to communicate her advice to aging women depressed by what they see in the mirror and unable to endure publicly revealing the physical signs of their aging: the advice is for them to stay home where loved ones will shelter them from the harsh reality of wrinkles and gray hair. She says, "If our looking-glasses tell us unpalatable truths we may always see ourselves at our best in the mirrors of loving and friendly eyes"; so, to enjoy an otherwise cold old age, "we must hug the closer the joys of the fireside" (10). Because women 90 years ago had a narrow domestic role prior to old age, with sexual attractiveness a major source of their power, not surprisingly they feared the loss of their looks and power as they aged. The effect of this concern over deteriorating appearance was to narrow a woman's horizons still further in her later years: following Mrs. Kingsland's advice (and that of others like her), she would refuse to display her crow's-feet and gray hair publicly. The underlying assumption is that the domestic sanctuary, not the risky wide world, is the only place where a woman ought to end her life.

Norman Hapgood, writing for the *Atlantic Monthly* in November 1903, in fact suggests that women's narrow domestic interests precipitate their aging before men (689). On the other hand, an article in *Chamber's Edinburgh Journal* in 1902 uses the same assumption about women's narrow domestic sphere and preoccupation with trivia to reach the opposite conclusion about women's longevity: woman's "capacity and love for continually talking about nothing has helped her materially toward length of days" because such conduct helps to circulate the blood without taxing the mind and the body unduly ("Happy Old Age" 198–99)! Whether extending or shortening their lives, however, women's narrow domesticity and consequent intellectual shallowness are both assumed and endorsed; old age is not envisioned as giving women the opportunity to develop themselves intellectually or to liberate them from their narrow domestic interests. And all three authors suggest the limited nature of women's general capacities, including the capacity to deal with aging. Moreover, they almost imply that it is women's fault for aging and for becoming unattractive. No wonder women developed the reputation of lying to the federal government's census takers about their age (see "Woman and the Age Question" 578–79, for example).

At the same time that these authors blame women for aging, they and others urge women to accept their aging and to "act their age" in a way that further restricts their freedom and seals them off from the world of youth. Avoid "youthful affectation," warns a writer in

Littell's Living Age in 1892 ("Old Men" 632). Similarly, Mrs. Kingsland and the author of "The Flying Years," Arthur T. Vance, are concerned that women age in a seemly manner, that is, not act young and adventuresome, but retire to the hearth. Mrs. Kingsland says it is most unseemly to imitate "juvenility" or covet "the prerogatives of youth" (10). Vance warns that the older woman should not "ape the dress of youth" although he gives equal time to old men's "foolishness"—"fatuous old gentlemen should [not] seek the society of maids" (17). It is not proper for the old to have the fun that the young have. Instead, they ought calmly "to enjoy seasonably the ripeness of life's fruit" (Vance 17). Here the image of ripening implies a narrower and more passive experience than the impassioned and philosophically inquiring period of ripening imagined by May Sarton and other writers of *Reifungsromane*. Passivity as the appropriate posture of elders is also implied in an 1894 *Atlantic Monthly* article by F. Sheldon: his tone is saccharine as he argues that "the Indian summer of life" should be reserved for the tranquil domestic pleasures of grandchildren, good food, and accumulated wealth (673).

While the usual tone of these warnings is mild and parental, a November 1, 1906, article in *The Nation*, "How to Grow Old," angrily and moralistically condemns active elders, male and female, who "artificially" try to recapture their youth:

> It is really not by the affectation of youth that old age is to preserve itself from degeneracy and senile imbecility. The sprightly old lady who dyes her hair, paints her face . . . and dresses like a debutante, the old *viveur* who believes that by keeping his youthful vices he conceals his advancing years [are out of step and reveal their] moral incapacity. (365)

Apparently threatened by elders' youthful "misconduct," the author tries to desex elders and compartmentalize youth and age, denying elders' capacity for the energy and *joie de vivre* of youth. All the articles suggest that mental and physical deterioration—"senile imbecility"—will sharply demarcate the old and the young.

A similar attempt to curtail elders' still vital energies, this time in the role of productive worker, occurs in a very ageist essay, "Youth vs. Age," that appeared in the March 19, 1898, edition of *The Spectator*: "We should not wonder if the world reconsidered one of its settled opinions, and began to doubt whether after all the old were so much more capable than the young. . . . They have lived in grooves, or in mental seclusion, or in work which cannot change." (402–3). This statement attempts to reverse the tradition of honoring the elderly that had prevailed for generations in England, and seems the rallying cry of the industrial and technological revolution's youthful leaders: the elderly cannot keep up with the changes happening around them, which greatly impairs their performance; hence, they should be retired to their firesides. The warning to the aged in this and other articles is clear and self-defensive: do not try to continue working, pursuing love and sexual fulfillment, like the young; act your age and condition—become virtually moribund. Authors like Clara Emily Harrison as late as 1920 still claim that the elderly "need quiet and rest" (428).

And is there any compensation for the surrender of youthful vitality in senescence? Yes, these articles offer some by creating a myth of the philosophical mellowness or tranquility of old age. In old age, claims the "How to Grow Old" article quoted earlier from *The Nation*, there is "a feeling of calm and freedom when the passions relax their hold" because "emotions are concentrated on higher things and infantile diffusions are avoided" (365). In Britain a writer for *The Spectator* expresses almost the same idea three years earlier, in 1903: "There is a perpetual serenity, a great calmness" not open to the young, "the peace of a prolonged twilight" before the night of death ("The Outlook" 567). These authors foresee in old age a balancing of the emotional keel, a dulling of our responses to pleasure and pain. As we lose the highs and lows of life, we gain a new perspective and sense of humor about the absurd struggles humankind endures on earth; by old age we learn "the true nature of the absurd, ridiculous, or grotesque" ("Old Men" 633). In other words, the articles suggest that we grow in wisdom as we age; this notion is in ironic juxtaposition with the other presumption that senile imbecility awaits us.

Only a couple of the early articles avoid extremes, saying that we do not change much in our personalities and outlook. One claims old people are not so different from themselves in youth, just more tired—a preview of the continuum concept of youth and age ("Old Men" 629). Another says people are more themselves in old age, anticipating the theme of elders' strengthened identity in *Reifungsromane* (Hapgood 688). Moreover, several articles do urge the elderly to remain active, mainly on the domestic front. Yet the Golden Pond myth of old age's calm, associated with the cessation of activity and intense emotional life, is more commonly evoked as the reward of a life well lived. I say it is a myth that old age offers mellow serenity because more recent, more realistic articles on and by old people describe the strong passions and turbulence of old age, as do the *Reifungsromane*.

What kind of climate might this popular journalism of 1890 to 1920 have created for readers and writers of fiction that dealt with aging? Perhaps the average reader would expect the stereotyped characters that keep recurring in the magazines: the aged dandy or the too merry old widow, the demented or foolish old person, the inactivated fireside knitter who has essentially given up. The reader might also look for the sentimentalizing of the end of life, a glossing over of the aches and pains as well as the agonies, the yearnings, the bitterness and the loneliness, in a Golden Pond haze—in contrast to the realistic and naturalistic turn that fiction was taking between 1890 and 1920. Such expected material might not seem too promising to an aspiring realistic writer who wanted to write truths about aging. Was the public ready for unpretty and passionate portrayals of the aged? Perhaps not. It is interesting that the history of fiction during these years does not reveal many central characters who are old or much emphasis on the passage into old age as a central theme of a work; on the other hand, youthful heroes and heroines abound, and their education into the ways of the world, their passage from youth into maturity, such as Dreiser's *Sister Carrie* (1900) and Joyce's *Portrait of the Artist as a Young Man* (1916), is a predominant focus of the fiction. The authors often stop their sagas of developing heroes and heroines at midlife, either with death, as for example Woolf's Mrs. Ramsey in *To the Lighthouse* (1927) and Chopin's *The Awakening* (1899), or with the promise of the golden haze in the future, as for example Cather's *My Ántonia* (1918). Authors during these years sometimes trace the history of a protagonist from youth to old age, but do not detail the aged person's interior life or the actual experience of aging; the Golden Pond haze, or the promise of one, often ends these works' histories of their protagonists. Some of D. H. Lawrence's novels illustrate this narrative pattern; the characters age, the generations pass, but Lawrence is more concerned with "the relationship between the generations, between man and woman . . . and . . . the proper basis for the marriage relationship" (Daiches and Stallworthy 2109)—when the characters are young or in their prime—than he is with the experience of aging.

The notion of old age as Golden Pond serenity or cozy security by the hearth is challenged in a 1920 article in *The Cornhill Magazine* in a way that anticipates the modern paradigm of the plight of the aged. The cynicism of the post–World War I years may have influenced the author as she observes that, despite Britain's system of old-age pensions, society increasingly needs old-age homes, institutions that contrast to nineteenth-century Britain's cruel abandonment of the elderly poor in workhouses. We cannot keep a Golden Pond/by the fireside notion of old age if families abandon elders in widowhood or widowerhood, even if old-age pensions aid in their support. The author, Clara Emily Harrison, states that with these pensions, people thought "that by the fireside in almost every house either grandfather or grandmother would find a place, but this soon proved a fallacy" (Harrison 428). These words herald the modern plight of the elderly in Britain, the United States, and Canada. Families were no longer welcoming the old into the domestic haven, perhaps in part because there were increasing numbers of them for families to support. This subject is addressed occasionally in magazines of the 1950's and 1960's and regularly in 1970's and 1980's articles. The Golden

Pond myth also begins to be challenged in the 1950's, 1960's, and 1970's, and the binary opposition between youth and age begins to weaken.

Some articles from the 1950's through the 1970's begin to recognize ageism and to reject the stereotype of the elderly as the antithesis of youth through individualized portraits of older people that resemble youth in their activities and activism. Some overt ageism still exists, as in an *Esquire* article that I will discuss, and some articles by elders display a defensive posture, especially in the late 1960's, the era of the generation gap and the youth culture. Yet a sympathy emerges for the economic and social plight of the old, at times reaching crisis proportions in the 1970's. The plight of the elderly was more and more in the limelight with cover stories in the 1970's in such widely read magazines as *Time*.

In such articles as this June 2, 1975, *Time* cover story, the metaphor of old age as cozy domestic retirement by the family fireside goes up in smoke. Instead of "spending their last years in peace and security, respected and cared for by their families and friends," the elderly face increasing uncertainty, isolation, and a struggle just to survive ("New Outlook" 44). In that article Dr. Robert Butler, the prominent geriatric specialist who coined the term *ageism*, declares that the process of growing old " 'has been made unnecessarily and at times excruciatingly painful, humiliating, debilitating, and isolating through insensitivity, ignorance, and poverty' " (47) because of the public's prejudice against elders. The article also suggests that the elderly may still be productive contributors to society if we let them; it cites an American Medical Association statement that there is "no evidence that older workers are any less efficient than younger ones" (48). Finally, the article projects a more positive future for the old by suggesting that many Americans are becoming newly motivated to alleviate the suffering of the elderly. The author notes that the militant Gray Panthers' increasing visibility and political clout will help to change the government's treatment of the old and to challenge the image of old age as vulnerable passivity.

An article by Martin Gumpert, M.D., that appears earlier (July 8, 1951) similarly undermines the image of old age as a winding down to inactivity. Gumpert denies the notion that the old are "inescapable victims of human decline" (61) by offering some new models of active and prominent elderly people whom he met in Europe, "pioneers of a future type of old person [who are] participating creatively in life as long as life lasts" (61). He scoffs at the polarity between youth and age as well as the image of age as Golden Pond stagnation, declaring that these people displayed a strong creative urge and "this sudden wave of emotions, this craving for knowledge and human growth"; he praises them for having entered an impassioned "second prime of life," in which they could truly ripen (63). He also points out similarities between these elders and the young. These aged Europeans possessed the same "need for human warmth, human contact, for being talked to" that younger people have (63). They lacked the cynical despair often attributed to the old and felt optimism and enthusiasm for the future as they, like youths, worked actively in the present. Gumpert's portrayal of these prominent elderly artists, philosophers, and politicians argues for "repatriating" the old into society, by its rhetorical method of humanizing and individualizing.

As more and more of these individual portraits were published, familiarizing readers with elders' thoughts and feelings, the binary opposition between youth and age decreased. So did the public's tolerance for stereotypes of the elderly. We can sense the public's increasing curiosity about who the old really are, what they think and how they feel, and hence their greater receptivity to fiction that depicts old protagonists and develops themes and images of aging. Whetted curiosity joins with the rapidly increasing numbers of aged readers—and authors—to increase the number of articles published on the vital old, the passionate old, the real old.

In the 1960's, when the youth culture reigned in the United States, magazines like the *Saturday Evening Post* and *Look* were featuring essays in which authors would reflect on their own experiences with aging, sometimes with more than mere clichés, to combat some of the younger generations' stereotyping of the old. The title of a *Look* article (October 17, 1967) will tell you something about the era in which it was written and the defensive tone of the author, Russell Lynes: "A Cool Cheer for Middle Age." Lynes counters youth's accusation that elders are "entirely removed from reality" by claiming that middle age is a wonderful time of life beyond "the pain of initial self-discovery" that youth suffers (45). Lynes suggests that middle age is a liberating time in which the individual, no longer so concerned with impressing his elders, can be himself more and enjoy life's pleasures more. The middle-aged person has earned "the right to feel that one is not impelled to attempt the impossible without sacrificing . . . the right to enjoy fully . . . the possible" (45). In middle age, we are realists who know our limitations, respect ourselves, and have a taste for pleasure, Lynes says (48). These themes of a liberating self-acceptance, a stronger sense of identity, and a greater pleasure in living are central to *Reifungsromane* about middle-aged women.

Jonathan Daniels frankly and defensively declares in the *Saturday Evening Post* on February 25, 1967, "I'm Old and I'm Glad." Daniels radically seeks to restore positive nuances to our language of aging and argues against using euphemisms like "senior citizen" for an old person. He is proud of his status and grateful for his "season" of life (8), so he will age openly. Language should both reflect and foster this openness. He does, however, trail off into that Golden Pond haze at the end of his article, saying that "mellowness is a possibility and a promise too" (14); this seems to be his weapon against the youth culture's denigration of old age. Yet by seeing old age as a mellowing, he falls into the old mythicizing, the softpedaling of old age that suggests a lingering ambivalence about aging, despite his modern pride in his years.

John Gregory Dunne also shows some ambivalence in his July 15, 1967, article, "Halfway Home." Dunne claims he feels happier than he did at 25 even though he no longer feels immortal (21). At 35, however, he has gained enough of a perspective on life to feel less sure about the answers to life's big questions: "Answers are the luxury of the very young and hopeful" (22). Dunne thinks it is hard enough merely to frame life's questions. He reexamines for his *Saturday Evening Post* readers the idea found in earlier periodicals that we acquire wisdom as we age; he questions the stereotyped idea that elders, having lived so long, have the answers to life's questions. Thus Dunne suggests that we may not change much as we travel along that continuum from youth into old age. He loosens one of Western culture's most persistent binary oppositions: foolish youth versus wise old age. His essay also anticipates the pattern of philosophical questioning and searching in old age that is a preeminent aspect of *Reifungsromane*.

Arguing for a reassessment of Americans' fears about aging is an optimistic article in the August 1975 issue of *Psychology Today*, titled "What We Expect and What It's Like: Problems of Old Age." In the article, Pam Moore reviews the findings of a poll taken by Lou Harris for the National Council on Aging: Americans expect old age to bring ill health, television watching, sitting and thinking, vulnerability to victimization by crime, and the cessation of sexual activity. Most of these expectations are not fulfilled, or certainly not to the degree we expect. The article points out Americans' longstanding prejudice against the elderly: the "biggest problem" of the old "may be the public's attitude toward them" (30). This prejudice asserts that the old are entirely different from you and me; old age is another planet distant from the world of youth, and elders are not quite human, almost aliens. This American prejudice may, in part, have been inherited from British literature. From Dickens's "Aged Ps" to the pathological Miss Havisham, from George Eliot's dried museum specimen Mr. Casaubon to Yeats's old man as "a paltry thing/A tattered coat upon a stick," British literature contains this imagery of the old as Other: foreign, inhuman, and ghastly. The Harris poll essay urges readers to counter these cultural influences and to rehumanize their conceptions of the old by establishing more ties between young and old: " 'Both young and old can and need to identify with other older Americans, rather than believing that the elderly have different energies, interests, capabilities, and concerns' " (30). *Reifungsromane* in the 1970's and 1980's also strive to foster this identification between young and old.

Similarities between youth and age are also emphasized in a *McCall's* article in November 1975, "You Are What You Were," by Janet Chen. Chen reports on a research study done by Henry S. Maas and Joseph A. Kuypers at the University of California, Berkeley. The team interviewed individuals at age 30 and then again at 70 and "found that those who were active and happy when they were younger remained active and happy as they aged" (40). The researchers concluded that aging does not radically change the personality and that senescence need not bring illness, loneliness, or depression (Chen 40).

The Maas-Kuypers study also rejects the image found in the 1900 *Ladies' Home Journal* article of old women retiring to the fireside to be comforted by their families in old age. Maas and Kuypers found instead that "women who had held jobs or led active social lives were happier in old age and better able to cope with the loss of husbands or children to care for" (40). The happiest elders were also those who could preserve "the capability to play"—implying that old age can be fun, that fun is not unseemly for the old, and that human beings, regardless of age, need to have fun. The study reflects American culture in the 1970's and early 1980's, the "Me Decade" and era of self-development, with elders claiming their rights to pleasure, diversion, and individual growth and thus dismantling the dichotomy between youth and age. This idea of fun in old age also appears in the media in movies like *Cocoon*. And *Reifungsromane* even more vehemently insist on this association of age with pleasure.

In addition to this need of elders to have fun, J. B. Priestley adds in his 1966 article, "Growing Old," for Britain's *New Statesman*, the need "to be needed." He argues that "the old can give as well as take" (161); the old can and want to contribute to society. Priestley rejects the image of senescence as retirement beside Golden Pond and would substitute for it the language of productivity.

For all these positive "proselytizing" articles in magazines of the 1950's through the 1970's that persuade readers to associate age with energy, optimism, and fun, there are as many negative articles that describe how to put off or camouflage the horror and ugliness of growing old ("Hate that gray? Wash it away!" Fade those ugly, telltale age spots!). Especially indicative of the remaining age prejudice in our culture are the allegedly humorous pieces about aging, such as an article in *Esquire* in April 1975. "How to Get Old and Do It Right" offers a list of do's and don'ts, "humorously" illustrated, to demonstrate how to avoid being an obnoxious old man or woman. While the article claims that there are hateful old people and good ones, it dwells on certain negative stereotypes of elders that we have already seen. The authors agree with children (all children? another stereotype) that "old people are ugly and icky, a pain in the neck, boring, useless, unbearable, deaf, and simply not pleasant to have around" because they make the young feel guilt and other unpleasant emotions. The article "humorously" advises readers on how to avoid becoming intolerable old people and misogynistically targets older women as especially likely to be antipathetic: do not wear too much makeup, do not whine but rage, acquire a big ego (the Me Decade speaking again), and avoid settlement in Florida (73). The article's humor reveals American culture's serious love affair with youth in the 1970's and our countenancing of tired, ugly notions about the elderly.

Magazines in the 1980's have not entirely eliminated ageism from their pages, but they have raised the public's consciousness about ageism, often sounding the alarm against it. Articles on the aged and the experience of aging have proliferated, with major or cover stories in such magazines as *Newsweek* and Canada's equivalent, *Maclean's*, as well as in magazines of regional and more liberal interests like *Southern Exposure* and *Ms*. Consistently, the trend in these articles has been to undermine the binary opposition between youth and age. The articles are less tolerant of stereotypes. They present aging as an exciting process of growth and self-discovery by printing autobiographies of old people and interviews with elders. Ageism still exists, but it is being diluted by some of these journalistic efforts.

Ageism is evident in the 1982 *McCall's* article by a woman who argues against voluntarily revealing her age, implying her sense of shame about aging. The author, Johanna Garfield, claims that stereotypes of age still exist and that she has experienced ageism by revealing her age, "so why ask for trouble?" (124). She claims telling your age is a form of boasting that resembles hiding "your age with face-lifts or teenage clothes" (124). She can see no cause for pride in one's age. In such a statement she accepts the prevailing age stereotyping and ageism. And we know *Esquire* has not changed much in its approach to the subject of aging when it prints essays like the one by Taki Theodoracopulos, "Your Time Is Up: At Thirty-five Even Playboys Have to Act Their Age" (May 1983). In it, the author admits he is no longer attractive to young women, but refuses "to think like a middle-aged person" (135)—as if such thinking might undermine a healthy vitality. He quotes Jonathan Swift's view that "no wise man ever wished to be younger," but then acknowledges his foolishness by wishing for youth. Readers feel his depression and self-dislike as he contemplates his aging.

Articles for female readers going through the passage to middle age assume a similar self-dislike; the issue of their fading appearance surfaces often in articles in women's magazines that proclaim what Margery Finn Brown says in a June 1982 *McCall's*: looks are more important to women in our society, so aging women mind losing their looks more than men do (66). This theme has appeared consistently since the 1900 "by the fireside" *Ladies' Home Journal* article. In November 1982 *McCall's* printed another article about why age shows faster in some women's faces than in others, and "why yours doesn't have to be one of them" (Heyn 117). The article offers sensible facts about health that may help a woman preserve her beauty, but nevertheless conveys a negative message about aging appearance: "While most of us aren't obsessive about staying young—even though our society makes it hard not to be—few of us want to age prematurely" (Heyn 164). The only difference between earlier negativism about aging and this contemporary message is that its tone is apologetically ageist. Yet in Britain, the magazine *She* ran an unapologetically ageist article in

February 1986 on "The Big Sag," aging skin, which the author compared distastefully to "an old bra . . . with greying, baggy straps and fastenings" (Voak 101). Articles like these that associate negative images with signs of aging in our own and others' bodies perpetuate a bias against looking and being middle-aged or old.

Middle age has, nevertheless, been positively treated in major magazine articles in recent years. In a *Newsweek* essay (February 14, 1983), "The Myths of Middle Age," author Sharon Begley tries to puncture depressing myths associated with middle age for women in America. Middle age does not have to be a confrontation with " 'empty-nest syndrome' " or " 'forty-year-old jitters,' " when in other cultures such as India women begin to enjoy "greater status, authority and freedom" (71). Begley argues that once their childbearing function is fulfilled, middle-aged women can experience a real blossoming of personality, with more time for their own pursuits and more opportunity to cultivate their assertiveness and independence. Begley seeks to reeducate Americans about their notions of middle-aged women's roles. Begley also notes a role reversal of men and women in middle age: while men in their late 40's begin to look forward to retiring, women in that age group take managerial jobs outside the home and experience new energy and autonomy (75). On a similar theme, although rather tongue in cheek, Libby Purves, in an article in Britain's *Punch*, describes the emergence of strong womanhood as traditional sexuality (femininity) diminishes, playing with the medical fact that after menopause the testosterone level in women increases, so that women become "more forceful and commanding . . . increasingly interested in roles where leadership is important" (11). Purves marvels at "postmenopausal indestructibility; the terrible beauty which is born out of the first heavy-going half-century of womanhood" (11). Just past 35 herself, Purves declares she will welcome menopause and "dream of world domination" (12). Readers inevitably think of Margaret Thatcher here as her nation's role model for the postmenopausal, politically powerful woman.

This notion of a middle age where women redirect their activities and develop their potential strengths becomes a central theme in *Reifungsromane* that focus on middle-aged heroines, such as Allison Lurie's *Foreign Affairs*, Gail Godwin's *A Mother and Two Daughters*, Mary Gordon's *Of Men and Angels*, and the fiction of Doris Lessing and Alice Adams. Magazine articles such as Begley's and Purves's inform readers of middle age's opportunities for women and also reflect the expanding interest in middle age of an increasingly middle-aged readership. Begley's article concludes that middle-aged American women can take heart "from the successes of their sisters in traditional societies" (75). The American public benefits from such cross-cultural comparisons of aging, which enable them to realize that attitudes toward aging are culturally determined and provincial, not innate, inevitable, and unchangeable.

Some recent articles more directly attack ageism by describing the symptoms of biased thinking about old age. *Ladies' Home Journal* shows how far it has come since 1900 by printing a remarkable essay about a 26-year-old woman who went "underground" as an elderly woman at least 200 times in 14 different states in the United States. Through costume and makeup, Patty Moore became an 85-year-old, and discovered that "the more I was perceived as elderly by others, the more 'elderly' I actually became" (Moore 46). Moore describes her experiences as an old woman, including the sense of being ignored, the frightening vulnerability to crime and jostling by rude people on city streets, the difficulty in negotiating street curbs not designed with the old in mind, and the neverending need to be held, touched, and loved in a society where others fear the old as they fear contagious diseases. Moore learns that the body may age, but that it is merely a prison in which a youthful inner self still exists (131). That lesson is central in the fiction of aging. What she did literally, many *Reifungsromane* enable a receptive reader to do vicariously through intense literary experiences.

In Katherine Barnett's interview with Moore for the article, titled "Old Before Her Time," she discusses the ageism with which Moore was confronted when under cover, and she presents Dr. Robert N. Butler's list of "six damaging myths of old age": it is sexless and mindless, useless and powerless; it is a disease rather than a natural, continuing process; and it makes all old people alike (Moore 48). Barnett raises our consciousness about these six "warning signs" of ageism—like cancer's seven danger signals—in order to fight the disease. Additional immunization against these myths of senescence is available through the individualized and humanized portraits of elders in *Reifungsromane*. While Moore experiences ageism herself, she also learns, as an "old" woman, a positive dimension of age that she describes to readers of *Ladies' Home Journal*: the feelings and desires of old women, including the desire for sex and love, often portrayed in heroines of *Reifungsromane*, like Taylor's Mrs. Palfrey, Pym's Marcia Ivory, and Sarton's Caro Spencer.

A major story in *Newsweek* (November 1, 1982) by David Gelman also attempts to undermine myths about the elderly by offering new role models of elders, which Daisy Grunau, a consultant on aging whom Gelman interviewed for the article, claims we need: " 'We are pioneers in aging, and we don't have any role models' " (Gelman 56). This article and others that interview or sketch portraits of active, vital elders dispel the rocking-on-the-front-porch model of old age and the diminished self-image that most of us anticipate. Besides describing the lives of active elders, Gelman examines Butler's stereotypes of old age, such as that it is sexless, commenting that despite "medical evidence that sexual activity can be normal even into the ninth decade of life," many think of sex for the old as unseemly; this attitude that elders should not have fun, including sexual fun, and that elders should "act their age," has been handed down from earlier magazine articles (57). Gelman attempts to dispel these stereotypes by presenting the youthful thoughts, feelings, and physical desires of the old such as those of 74-year-old Grunau: " 'We adult citizens . . . are thinking and feeling forty so much of the time. Then you look into the mirror and you get a shock' " (58–59). The shock is that the body has aged while the mental outlook remains youthful; hence, "acting one's age" becomes problematic. This mirror imaging of an elder often appears in *Reifungsromane* within similar "shock-of-recognition" scenes that convey the tension between youthful mental outlook and aging physical appearance.

Gelman's article, through its portraits of mentally vigorous seniors, posits that the old can contribute to society. Gelman quotes Dr. George Pollack, director of Chicago's Institute for Psychoanalysis, in an attempt to repatriate and rehumanize the old: readers must remember that elders " 'are people who continue to have hopes, dreams, desires, who get terribly angry and no longer have work to vent their aggression on—and who want still to be useful to the people around them' " (60). Gelman preaches at the end of his article against the stereotyping of the old and urges these "full-timers" to "assert their continued humanity in a culture that hails old age as an achievement and treats it as a failure" (60). If American culture still harbors hostility to the old, writers like Gelman are challenging it and working to dissolve the barriers between youth and age.

Helping to encourage departures from our depressing associations with aging are some wonderful individual portrayals of seniors in magazines from *McCall's*, *Maclean's*, and the *Saturday Evening Post* to *Ms.* and *Southern Exposure*. These portrayals stress elders' comfort in being themselves, as well as their new creative freedom and political self-expression; the world of youthful activity is reopening to these seniors. Britain's popular romance novelist, Barbara Cartland, is the focus of a January–February 1985 story in the *Saturday Evening Post*, "Getting Older, Growing Younger," in which she derides the familiar myth of old age, "the old-fashioned idea of 'Granny likes to sit by the fire knitting' or 'old people need peace and quiet' " (63). She actively works, writing, speaking, and traveling, and she always has new projects to look forward to. Her message is, simply, that age is in the mind (not in the skin and hair). Cartland's enthusiasm and vitality are matched by Margery Finn Brown in a June 1982 *McCall's* article, "Do You Mind Not Being Young?" Brown's answer to this question is a resounding "No!" She sounds a theme about the older woman increasingly prevalent in American culture, that old age brings the opportunity for a woman to be herself: "I like myself more, I am myself in old age as I was not, as I could never have been, in youth or middle age" (66); and "One of the joys of being old is that I feel no obligation to wear myself out being more agreeable or more tactful than I actually am" (64). The older woman can realize potentialities that were ignored over the years because some inhibitions, internally and culturally imposed, have been eliminated from her life: whether her conduct is to others "unseemly," "unmotherly," "unwifely," or "unfeminine" no longer rules the older woman. Relying more on her own views than on others', she can give her feelings free rein, which means that old age can bring stronger passions, not the mellow or numbed feelings that the Golden Pond myth presumes. Says Brown, "I expected it [old age] to be smoother, more serene, less passionate. . . . I'm more touched by joy and sadness" (Brown 66). While she may not have youth's sense that "all is possible," she does have energy, "zest, [and] curiosity" (Brown 64–65; 66).

This older woman is the stuff from which good fiction is now developing: she is vital and passionate; she has a complex history; she is bound for self-discovery and self-cultivation, like the youthful culture around her; and within her is the pathos of wanting to live richly for a limited amount of time remaining. She is what Caroline Bird characterizes as an "S.O.W.," a "Salty Old Woman" in an article that appeared in *Ms.* in August 1983. The S.O.W. is sensual, experiencing affection for her own body and a newfound sexuality, and flexible, making major changes in her life regularly, as well as courageous—publicly outspoken. While she looks forward to something new in her life each day, she is also realistic. The S.O.W., observes Bird, is going through the "second blooming" that Agatha Christie describes, where energies from nurturing children and other personal relationships are rechanneled into nurturing ideas, causes, and the arts; this theme is addressed in such *Reifungsromane* as Paule Marshall's *Praisesong for the Widow*, where Avey Johnson becomes a proud extender of her ethnic heritage. Whereas in the past fiction writers were often drawn to the "first blooming" of characters passing into adulthood in *Bildungsromane*, now the "second blooming" is acquiring appeal for writers and readers. Like *Ms.*, the British magazine *She* presents a portrait of a vigorous and nonconformist elder, Maria Reiche, an 81-year-old anthropologist still at work in the Peruvian desert. Such journalism whets the public's appetite for fiction about S.O.W.'s.

The pages of the May–June 1985 issue of *Southern Exposure* are also filled with salty old women and men. The editors' aim in this issue is "to combat ageism by offering positive profiles of Southern elders" ("Older, Stronger, Wiser" 10). They do so with stories about elders who are political and social activists fighting elder abuse. They also portray the organizers of events celebrating aging and old age, such as Old Peoples' Day in Eighty-Eight, Arkansas, and the Croning ceremony initiated by a group of 50-year-old women in Florida who want to reclaim the word "crone" for its associations with endurance, wisdom, and experience. As crones, they strive to regain self-respect and pride in their years. The cumulative message of the issue is that these elders are realizing their full potential and rediscovering themselves. A biographical piece on the late Barbara Deming by Mab Segrest puts it this way, "The older she grew, the more she became herself" (72). And an excerpt from the journal of Florida Scott-Maxwell, published in 1968, tells us once again about the bubbling passions of the old. She describes her own 70's as serene, but her 80's as passionate with moral fervor and the longing "to put things right" (19). She shows us that life can end with a neat sense of closure, but also that one can live fully, despite sorrows, unreliable bodies, and thoughts of death, till the very end: "I want to tell people approaching and perhaps fearing age that it is a time of discovery" (20).

Canadian culture is making similar inroads against ageism. In a January 17, 1983, cover story for *Maclean's*, "Canada's Weekly Newsmagazine," the author Val Ross presents old age as a time of discovery by including portraits of salty, vital elders, discussing "XYZ," the "Extra Years of Zest" club, where some 80-year-olds try swimming for the first time and others attend university classes.

As Ross says, "The life that many of Canada's older citizens are shaping for themselves is vigorous, regenerative, even fulfilling" (24). While she also writes about the monetary crunch that will inevitably come in Canada's efforts to care for the elderly and about the rise in alcoholism and suicide among the old, Ross's article positively portrays athletic elders and describes exciting alternative life-styles for the old, such as living in communes and in college dormitories with other students (27). In such settings and activities, the binary opposition between youth and age begins to break down, and such articles as Ross's assist in this breakdown.

These 1980's magazines, with their lively portraits of vital elders, have whetted the public's appetite for more literary conversations with old people. They have diminished our fear of the old and our fear of our own aging while deepening our curiosity about aging, which increasing numbers of readers will face. Popular journalism has recorded some of the thoughts and feelings of the old and introduced new images and themes of aging. The barriers between younger and older are crumbling, and readers of all ages are ripe for the more complex literary experience with aging offered in *Reifungsromane* written during the 1960's, 1970's, and 1980's. The emergence of this genre may well represent a watershed in literary and social history.

2

Beginning the Journey to Selfhood in Middle Age

"Middle-age spread," "fat and forty," "middle-age depression," "empty nest syndrome," "middle-age crisis," "lonely middle-aged widow": these stereotypical associations with middle age suggest stagnation; the loss of physical vitality, attractiveness, and usefulness to others; diminishing self-pride; and increasing isolation. Americans, Britons, and Canadians may attempt to slough off the negatives with redoubled efforts at jogging and aerobic exercise classes or with jokes about dieting, facelifts, and hair color, but despair often hovers behind the sweating and the levity.

In contrast, much contemporary fiction by women is challenging these stereotypes by helping readers to see the potential in middle age for discovery and new activities, for continuing the *reifung*, or emotional and philosophical ripening begun in youth. *Reifungsromane* enable readers to experience vicariously the lives and thoughts of middle-aged heroines who grow in self-knowledge and energy and change the direction of their lives. The London-based Doris Lessing has created two such middle-aged heroines in Kate Brown of *The Summer Before the Dark* (1973) and Jane Somers of *The Diaries of Jane Somers* (1983). The San Francisco–based Alice Adams explores American versions of the adventurous middle-aged heroine in three short stories from *To See You Again* (1982). Both authors present middle age as a time to take to the open road, often literally, when their heroines discover who they are and where they want to go for the rest of their lives. Both authors also undermine the polarity between youth and age by presenting "youthfully" passionate and active middle-aged women.

DORIS LESSING'S *THE SUMMER BEFORE THE DARK* AND *THE DIARIES OF JANE SOMERS*

The *Reifungsroman* is purposefully, self-consciously adopted as a genre by Doris Lessing in *The Summer Before the Dark* and the two novels contained in *The Diaries of Jane Somers*, *The Diary of a Good Neighbor* and *If the Old Could*. . . . The analyses of Lessing's *Reifungsromane* that follow note the ethics and vision conveyed in Lessing's fiction as well as the linguistic and structural features of the genre, an approach urged by two Lessing critics, Annis Pratt and L.S. Dembo; they argue that "the prophetic dimension of her works precludes too narrowly aesthetic an analysis, since they are not written for our artistic delight but to warn of satanic mills and to suggest a New Jerusalem" (Pratt and Dembo xi). In other words, this chapter focuses on Lessing's development of an important subgenre of the contemporary novel, but also explores Lessing's warning about cultural misperceptions of women's old age and her prophecy of an ageless utopia.

Lessing prophesies that far from being a "dark" period of a woman's life (*The Summer Before the Dark* uses the word ironically in the title), old age is a time of "sun-drenched" spiritual growth and increasing self-appreciation, heralding a kind of New Jerusalem—which she radically attributes, in the earlier novel, to the freedom that comes from shedding one's sexuality. That loss of sex appeal that aging women usually dread because it curtails their power in society Lessing enables readers to see, instead, as a liberating and empowering divestiture. This divestiture redefines a woman's identity by placing her in a new world beyond gender and age. In *The Diaries of Jane Somers*, Lessing also fosters linkage between middle age and old age, the continuum advocated by feminist critic Paula A. Treichler (61). This continuum enables "ageless" readers to face aging and death, to develop self-respect and receptivity to elders, and to acknowledge the capacity for pleasure, regardless of age. Her optimistic message, conveyed through portraits of Kate Brown and Jane Somers, will convert many a reader for whom "old age looms ahead like a calamity" (de Beauvoir 13).

Imagine you are an attractive, intelligent 45-year-old mother of four, married to a successful doctor and efficiently managing a busy household in suburban London. Your husband and grown children are away for the summer. The summer beckons you to adventure, to introspection, to consideration of the rest of your life. Do you panic at the crossroads? Do you sink into the "empty nest" in a self-pitying depression? Not if you are Kate Brown. During this crucial summer, Kate literally and psychologically takes a journey; psychologically she faces the chill wind from the north, the novel's initial metaphor for old age, reflecting Kate's fears about her future. Kate later finds old age is not so chill after all. Literally, Kate has a middle-aged woman's summer experiences with a job, a lover, a trip in Spain, a draining illness, and a transformative convalescence. These experiences—together with an evolving dream life, a common element of *Reifungsromane*—enable Kate to understand her middle age, to have a foretaste of old age, and to conceptualize age as a continuum, not as the pole opposite youth. Because readers become engaged in Kate's odyssey, they also become middle-aged and preview old age.

Lessing's narrator indicates at the beginning of *The Summer Before the Dark* that she has created a variation on the *Bildungsroman*, describing the story about to unfold as a process of "learning how to grow old," that "successor and repetition of the act of growing up" (5). This growing-old process repeats, but also extends the growing-up process because the growing-up process for women so often results in vague, half-formed identities. Lessing suggests her heroine's indefinite identity by not even naming her until the fifth page of the novel; designated simply as "a woman," Kate Brown becomes everywoman, who must through introspection return to her half-formed self prior to the years of marriage and motherhood when her self-development had been suspended, in order to reactivate that development and shape her future. The story of Kate's aging, a specific case history of a journey undertaken by everywoman, is thus "representative as well as idiosyncratic"—a typical feature of both *Bildungsromane* (Rose 10; Buckley 6) and *Reifungsromane*.

On her journey, Kate leaves behind her role as "Mrs. Michael Brown," becoming a less sexual aging woman and previewing the autonomy and strength a woman can have in old age, not often experienced in married life. This preview of senescence allows her to reinterpret outworn attitudes about age and youth, which are reflected during the book's first six pages in the clichéd language, "the words and phrases as worn as nursery rhymes," which she almost ritualistically chants—and Lessing italicizes—expressions such as, "*I am not as young as I once was*" or "*Youth is the best time of your life*" (1; cf. 3–6). Probing clichés about aging as she probes the distorting language that has framed her memories of marriage and family, she gradually understands what her life has become and moves beyond her past, seeing in old age what Mary Ann Singleton describes as "something within herself that is eternal" (162–63) and something ageless in the universe as well. In this *Reifungsroman*, Kate learns what growing old means physically, psychologically, and spiritually.

As in the female *Bildungsroman*, much of Kate's journey is internal, involving her conscious will, her dreams, her sexual promptings, and her changing emotions. Her searching for self-knowledge and a new future is evident in the series of questions that regularly punctuate her inner monologues, often interrupting sentences. It is also evident in her frequent self-appraisal, from a third-person limited omniscient perspective, as she stands before the mirror that is a central image of *Reifungsromane*. In contrast to the journey in the female *Bildungsroman*, however, Kate's journey is also externalized, ranging over Turkey, Spain, and London, and is a liberating, not a restricting education leading to maturity. Kate's journey resembles the classic *Bildungsroman* in that she begins by making a couple of "false starts" (Howe 4) on this journey to old age. Yet she turns from them to attain an integrated identity and relationship with the world beyond age and gender, a calm self-assurance in facing old age, and the wisdom not to countenance false role playing. The older Kate is less reliant on family or society for approval and happiness than are such young adult heroines as Austen's Anne Elliott and Eliot's Dorothea Brooke. Lessing's novel suggests that in Western culture a woman has greater opportunity and capacity to grow old successfully than she does to grow up and that growing old usually enables one fully to grow up.

Annis Pratt makes an insightful parallel between the heroine of the *Bildungsroman* and the aging heroine, which applies to Kate: "For the woman past her 'prime,' as for the young hero not yet approaching hers, visions of authenticity come more easily than to women in the midst of their social experience" (*Archetypal* 11). As Kate steps beyond the "domestic enclosure" that has now become an "empty nest," she is at age 45 creating her vision of personal authenticity and preparing to embrace it.

The two false starts that begin Kate's movement toward personal authenticity involve Kate's attempts to remember and reinvent her lost youth, her sexual, premarital self, by securing a job and having a brief affair with a younger man. Both experiences keep Kate in her nurturing-mother role and stymie personal growth. Fortunately, however, these experiences occur when Kate has the space and time for introspection about her premarital self.

Lessing allows readers to experience Kate's summer of sometimes painful introspection by laying bare her thoughts through the narrator, whose omniscience is limited to the life of Kate's psyche. Although there are external events in Kate's life during the summer, including her job as a translator and conference organizer, her travels, and her interactions with new people, these events take up little of the narrative. Instead, with the narrator's guidance, readers follow Kate's analysis of her past and her present inner life, observe Kate's probing of her false "official memories" (90, 148), and witness her metaphorical purging of her past self as she endures an intestinal illness. Often images of raw exposure, bone stripped of skin (90, 138) or an animal being flayed alive, convey the brutal pain of her self-revelation and self-discoveries (19, 23, 46). Through the illness, intermittent reminiscences, and frequent self-analysis, all of which sabotage the linear movement of the plot, Lessing writes the aging woman's body and mind: the body's loss of resilience after illness and depletion of a carefully preserved sexual attractiveness; the mind's increasing recursiveness and the intermittent blurriness of borders between perceived reality and introspective fantasies. This narrative pattern enables readers to travel with Kate along the age continuum.

In addition to the narrative structure, two devices chart the psychological and philosophical changes in Kate: her changing hair styles and the series of dreams about a seal. Before the mirrors of the *Reifungsroman*, Kate observes her graying, increasingly disheveled hair (160). The seal is suggestive of Kate's alter ego and later in the dream sequence reveals her increasing ability to care for Kate Brown, as she leaves behind her maternal self and meets her pared-down self. The seal and Kate's dreams are a major aspect of Lessing's *Reifungsroman*, symbolizing the heroine's new self-knowledge and self-nurturing as well as her conceptualization of aging as a continuum and her acknowledgment of the proximity of old age and death.

Seeking her other selves, Kate abandons the empty nest to examine her options while renting a Woolfian room of her own in London. Her new job as a Portuguese translator at an international conference for Global Food Company inspires her to change her hairdo from soft housewifely waves, carefully designed to reflect her position in an upper-middle-class suburb, to the dark red, sensuous silkiness of her youth, indicating an inchoate change in her self-perception. Kate is moving beyond her children's objection to her expressing her nature—including the sensuous and the sexual; she need not be reduced to the maternal self. She also analyzes her feelings about her husband's extramarital affairs and realizes that by accepting them, "her own worth, even her substance, had been assaulted" (64). Through the years Kate has become inauthentic by giving pieces of herself away to husband

and children; this summer she ends such inauthenticity as her hair moves from housewifely waves, to sensuous mane, to uncontrolled, naturally gray bushiness.

Reassessing the empty nest phenomenon, Kate learns that not only do her husband and children no longer need her, but also that she no longer needs them to maintain self-worth. Yet, to eliminate her dependency on them for self-validation, Kate must meet her old age as a different woman, commit herself to experiences that will radically change her: "you got changed by being made to live through something and then you found yourself changed" (95). The "something" that she lives through, the summer's journey to her future as a stronger, more independent old woman, Kate initially fears will be a mere "dwindling away from full household activity into getting old" (8). Yet the process, rather, is a broadening one, enabling Kate to recognize elders' stamina and capacity for change, traits normally associated with youth.

To prepare for senescence, Kate must first mentally journey to her past: "The future would continue from where she left off as a child" since the years in between seemed to betray her real nature (125–26). Her years of marriage and childrearing have created the inauthentic Kate. Her job translating Portuguese inaugurates this mental journey backward to the more authentic, if younger and less mature Kate. Being part Portuguese, when she hears and uses the language again, Kate is besieged by memories of her youth, her one-year visit with her Portuguese grandfather, and her great social successes with young men. Her intensely sexual attractiveness and her Portuguese traits are elements of her identity that have been deflected since her marriage.

Although this two months' job at Global Food is important for reacquainting Kate with these aspects of her self, the job is also a false start on her journey to old age because her duties as a conference organizer in London and Istanbul have kept her in her usual role of nurse or mother (29). She must move beyond this maternal role of supplying "some kind of invisible fluid or emanation, like a queen termite . . . making a whole of individuals . . . a 'family' " (45) because she and her circumstances have outgrown this role.

Kate must also travel beyond her youthful sexual identity in order to face old age and give birth to her precious elderly self. Her elderly self will depart from this reenactment of her youthful self, especially from her sexual attractiveness, rediscovered and wielded while she is working at Global Food. Kate's second false start is her testing out of this rekindled sexual power in a brief liaison with Jeffrey Merton. It is a false start because he is thirteen years younger than she, which again elicits her maternal behavior, and because the sexual component of the liaison impedes her commitment to find a private room, "sit quietly, and let the cold wind blow as hard as it would" (68). While in Spain with him, she realizes that her sexuality, so painstakingly cultivated for her husband, is not a part of her authentic aging self because this sexual power reinforces her social role of catering to others' needs, not her own. Lessing suggests here that women are better off without the sexual apparatus, that it is not a source of women's true personal power as patriarchy has led us to believe—one's own unencumbered persona is—and that the cultivation of one's sexual appeal may limit a woman's growth and identity. A sexless and ageless society would more effectively promote and safeguard human integrity.

Lessing's suggestion that the older woman divest herself of sexual encumbrances to empower herself parallels the attitudes of many cultures that repose great confidence in older women's capacities for thought and leadership, granting postmenopausal women a much higher and more respected position in society than women of childbearing age. The essay by Libby Purves in *Punch*, mentioned in the previous chapter, embraces this notion of strong womanhood beyond sexuality (or beyond traditional femininity) by seizing on the medical fact that after menopause the testosterone (male hormone) level in women increases, so that women become more ambitious and forceful, exhibiting strong leadership qualities and aims. Only half facetiously, Purves marvels at "the post-menopausal indestructibility; the terrible beauty" of older women (11).

Lessing is giving us a more earnest version of this message about sexual "divestiture" through her portrayal of Kate's experimentation with using and then shedding her sexual powers during her transitional summer.

Kate's illness in Spain initiates the relinquishing of this sexual power and compels her to return to London, where her illness and convalescence bring the introspection necessary to achieve psychic wholeness. After an amniotic "underwater time" (139), she gives birth to an old woman, who, ironically, at first eats baby food and is prone to childish tantrums to gain attention, but who later acquires honest self-knowledge, maturity, integrity, and a dignified asexuality. The pattern of self-censorship and avoidance of truths (" 'There's something . . . I simply will not let myself look at . . . /Now/, look at it all' " 12) displayed in the first chapter is ended. She finally acknowledges her repressed grief and anger toward her family, and as Betsy Draine has pointed out, the intense, concentrated "experiencing of these emotions rapidly ages her face and her body" (125). Yet she wears these signs of aging with pride because they reveal that Kate is acquiring spiritual maturity. In fact, a newly resilient, but also firm and wise Kate Brown is emerging, who rejects the old dualities of youth (power) and age (passivity).

The new changes in Kate's hair reflect this emerging aspect of herself, her acceptance of old age, and the provisions she is making for old age. While in Spain, a band of gray hair challenges the dye. This band of gray widens and becomes bushier—more assertive— through her convalescence in London, reflecting a self that is no longer artificially sexual. She has traveled beyond the fragmented roles of middle-aged mother and carefully groomed, sexually dutiful wife to an integrated vision of her many selves, reflected in her hair, an identity beyond role playing and no longer "functioning at the level of conditioned responses to the world" (Kaplan 11). By presenting a vision of Kate's many selves, Lessing may be implying that the ability to contact a single "real self" is merely a myth, one that has been propagated by literary modernism. Postmodern feminist thinkers tend to conceptualize female identity as multiplicity of selves and insist on diversity in womanhood; Toril Moi, for example, posits "the true heterogeneity of women's powers" (125) while Julia Kristeva believes there are "as many 'feminines' as there are women" (Moi 169). Lessing also seems interested in emphasizing the complexity or multiple dimensions of Kate's female persona.

The complex, aging Kate decides not to court men's attention by disguising her age with hair dye and waving lotions. When she recovers her health and good looks, she retains the lesson she has learned about appearance and sexual power; she chooses not to "set" her "inner thermostat" in order to "attract men's sex" (205). She no longer needs to seek the sexual notice of men to be self-satisfied. She has progressed along the age continuum during her "long interior journey" (226), and now her self-concept and her appearance are more integrated: "The grey band . . . was going to stay. 'Oh no,' Kate heard herself muttering, as she looked at the grey, encouraging it to . . . banish the dye with the truth . . . 'never again, I must have been mad' " (232).

Through her hair Kate vows that she will never again allow herself to be inauthentic or fragmented by the demands of people and societal roles. A carefully cultivated youthful sexuality, she has learned, will broadcast to those around her—men, women and children—that she may be manipulated and led to self-dishonesty and fragmentation. Keeping her vow of integrity, which for Kate means fostering an ascetic plainness and rejecting the power to manipulate sexually, she can move into old age with equanimity and self-pride. Not changing her hair is a guarantee of this vow.

Readers learn the lesson about sexual power with Kate as she devises an experiment during her convalescence that is also her education in becoming a less sexual, less artificial elder. We watch her as she watches herself in the mirror while donning a properly fitting dress and twisting her hair up in a way society considers seductive. Then we see her strolling down a street, receiving appreciative attention from construction workers and other men in a park. Finally, she takes the same walk bushy-haired and loosely garbed, not conforming to society's dictates about how a middle-aged woman should look, and she is virtually invisible. Patty

Moore experienced the same invisibility in her experiment as an elderly woman, described in the *Ladies' Home Journal* article in the previous chapter. Kate finds she likes being invisible. Like Caroline Bird, the salty old woman in the *Ms.* article, Kate feels relieved of the burden of having to attract men sexually.

Readers who might in another context wonder how Kate could neglect her appearance so shockingly nod approvingly at her gray bushiness because it is the liberating passport into new modes of living. Readers change along with Kate while reading the novel so that hair dye and curlers hiding and taming gray hair no longer seem a sensible way of keeping the "enemy old age well at bay" (40); indeed, keeping old age at bay no longer seems sensible. As Lessing's novel directly "names" the old woman, undermining Anglo-American culture's notion of the old woman as Other, readers learn that youth and middle age are not very different from or any better than old age; old age simply provides more latitude for self-intensification. The saga of Kate's hair inspires in readers an attitudinal change about age, a rejection of popular culture's usually negative portrayals of older women.

Thus Kate relinquishes sexual attractiveness: its dividends in pleasure and its ultimately self-demeaning power; its burdens of sexual obligations to her husband, time and money obligations to her beautician; and its humiliating falseness to her natural persona. As Patricia Meyer Spacks has observed, Kate attains a sense of freedom by no longer needing the power of sexual appeal and by violating accepted standards of attractiveness (373). Lessing evidently believes that we, especially women, operate through our "biology," but that we may undermine biology's authority by aging into asexuality; through Kate, she suggests that aging offers a "mystical menopause that ushers in . . . self-knowledge" (Hendrin 85). The unsexed older woman can separate her self from her appearance, that which has in the past brought her validation from society. Shedding this sexual "equipment" by aging is a wonderfully liberating sensation, says Lessing: "It really is a most salutary and fascinating experience to go through, shedding it all. Growing old is really extraordinarily interesting" (quoted by

Hendrin 85). Lessing convinces readers that shedding one's sexuality is salutary through Kate's experiments with invisibility among the male construction workers; what woman ogled and hooted at by construction crews would not understand Kate's feeling of jubilation at such invisibility?

Kate also sheds the inhibitions imposed by the language that shapes traditional gender roles. Kate creates a new signifying space of language as the narrative flashes back to her "cow sessions"—consciously opposed to "bull sessions"—with her unconventional friend Mary. She recalls how they demolished the sacred cows of their social roles as women by howling with derisive laughter at a litany of words like "family," "home," "husband," "mother," and "father"; the narrator calls it "a ritual . . . in which everything their lives are dedicated to upholding is spat on" (150). Kate's guilt at this irreverence fades as the words are gradually demystified with the help of her young roommate Maureen, whose probing questions about men, marriage, and family punctuate their dialogue in the last chapter. Eventually Kate feels free to label conventional words like *love* as "a load of shit," moving beyond self-censorship (200) and understanding the politics of language, how people "use and [are] used by words" (244). Instead of speaking in clichés, as in the opening pages of the novel, and carefully measuring her words, giving different small parcels of self-expression to different people, a unified Kate can finally disclose freely to one person, Maureen, anything about everything she has been thinking, feeling, remembering, and dreaming about her life (245). As feminist poet Marge Piercy would say, Kate finally "unlearns to not speak."

That Kate achieves freedom, integrity, and acceptance of her aging self is not only apparent in her hair and language, but also in the outcome of her seal dreams. These dreams both chart the progress of her developing older self and further its development. In her dreams she carries a wounded, apparently dying seal through a severely cold climate and rough terrain, a region of death. She also faces other obstacles in the dreams, including a king, probably representing her husband, who rejects her for a younger woman, and vicious animals, possibly her children, that threaten to attack the seal. Betsy Draine thinks these parts of the dream suggest that Kate's husband and children may resent her emerging new identity (125). But more important, Kate fears their resentment, a fear that gradually diminishes. The dream journey, marked by the "loneliness and difficulty of her struggle north into the cold dark" (231), reflects her waking journey toward old age and death. Movement along the age continuum is cold, dark, fearful, full of painful lessons about role playing and self-reliance, but the destination is warm and filled with light. Telling Maureen about the dream, especially as she shifts her narrative viewpoint from third to first person (209), compels Kate to lose her detachment, engage completely with the dream, feel its force, and bring it to closure.

Kate finally carries the seal to its haven, the sea. The seal is grateful, full of renewed vitality and hope, when it sees other seals basking in the sun and cavorting in the water. As Kate saves the seal in the dream, so she saves her self by the end of the summer from disintegration and a death-bringing inauthenticity. Depositing this seal in the sea suggests that Kate has freed herself from her consoling role and turned to self-nurturing (205). She is invigorated by the sense that she has the world before her; like Maureen, she has many choices.

As Kate watches the seals, she observes, significantly, that the sun is "in front of her, not behind . . . a large, light, brilliant, buoyant, tumultuous sun that seemed to sing" (267). The warmth and light ahead of her suggest that this is a moment of triumph as well as of hope for Kate after her struggle in the dark during the summer; the book's title reflects Kate's initial misunderstanding about old age and about what the summer would bring for her—after the dark struggle toward old age, old age itself is enlightening for her. Kate foresees not only a brighter old age, but also a brightness beyond death as a consequence of her interior journey. The breezes of eternal spring fan the seals. In addition, Singleton notes that there is a "suggestion of eternity" in the rebirth and sun imagery at the end of Kate's dream and that her introspective journey has enabled Kate to glimpse "something within herself that is eternal . . . a unity . . . , an emerging spirituality" (162–63). The glimpse of the eternal within herself and her intimation of eternity after death allay Kate's fears about old age and death. Kate may also be glimpsing some eternal higher state of mind beyond the self, as Sydney Janet Kaplan suggests, a " 'transpersonal' " state related to Lessing's interest in Sufism, where the self is " 'larger, more cosmic, less personal' " and eliminates the "burden of personality" represented in the seal (Kaplan 6–7). This state has the same ideal quality as the new signifying space for mind and body imagined by Kristeva, where identity based on gender disintegrates at its core. Lessing's prophesying power enables Kate and the reader to envision through Kate's dreams an edenic spiritual state in life after middle age and, after death, an ageless utopia.

The seal dreams serve one other very important function: they systematically draw readers into Kate's thought processes, conscious and unconscious, urging readers to guess what will happen in the next installment of this "cliffhanging" story and asking them to interpret the symbolism behind each event, character, and changing terrain in the dream (is Freud being gently spoofed here?). Readers become absorbed in putting the pieces of this dream puzzle together to form a meaningful whole—which often slips "deconstructively" away—and they long for satisfying closure in the last installment of the dream, in the same way that Kate works to put together the discrete pieces of her life in a new, more meaningful whole by the end of the summer, creating the perspective and the life she wants for her old age. Readers look forward to these dream segments as welcome interruptions of the "daytime" plot because they permit more intensive vicarious experiencing of Kate's psychological journey. The dream's recurrences and the repetition of its symbols in modified forms and contexts show readers that Kate is changing. Moreover, the seal increasingly speaks to readers as an endearing creature worthy of care, affection, and rescue. In the same way, Kate begins to feel more and more that her own persona is lovable, durable, and deserving of nurture and protection. The seal dreams give readers an intense literary experience of Kate's psyche as it confronts old age. Readers are likely, at the final installment of the seal dream, to feel a catharsis only a little less exquisite than Kate's.

Thus Kate proudly embraces her graying, independent self. She no longer relies on the approval of husband and family for her feelings of self-worth, no longer conforms to societal demands and assumptions regarding her appearance, behavior, and attitude toward aging. She has put away role playing, she has attained an unshakable sense of herself, and she joyfully anticipates old age. Lessing teaches us through Kate's story what old age means. It means the opportunity to become reacquainted with oneself, to reintegrate neglected aspects of oneself, and to pursue with a sense of excitement and hope changes in behavior that will build and safeguard personal authenticity. It is a rare opportunity to attain the self-respect that Joan Didion describes as a coming home to one's self. Such self-respect gives a person the courage to take risks and accept full responsibility for her life (142–48). This is a far cry from the plight in which most *Bildungsromane* leave their half-formed heroines. In this *Reifungsroman*, the heroine fully ripens so that she can finally go *home*—the last word of Lessing's novel, resonant with new meanings—as an older woman of integrity.

Lessing's fascination with the experience and the novel of aging does not end with the publication of *The Summer Before the Dark* in 1973. A decade later, in a book that in many ways parallels and in some ways parodies or "deconstructs" *The Summer Before the Dark*, she writes about a middle-aged heroine, Jane Somers (a pun on "summer"?), who learns to face squarely her middle age and future old age through that of Maudie Fowler, a woman past 90 who becomes Jane's substitute mother. First published pseudonymously under the rubric of Jane Somers's autobiographical diary as a hoax against the publishing industry, *The Diary of a Good Neighbor*, with Lessing behind a double mask, parodies Lessing's earlier novel by depicting in Jane an initially less than sympathetic character who is the opposite of Kate Brown: she is as self-centered as a childless, recently widowed, attractive 49-year-old can be; obsessed with her own immaculate, studied grooming and attire in a way that mocks Kate's decision to maintain a natural appearance; entirely focused on a publishing career that she knows she does well; unnurturing; and a cowardly woman, by her own admission. Her cowardice, her inability to deal with her husband Freddie's and her mother's terminal cancers, leads her into many unkindnesses toward them, including emotional withdrawal from them and guilt-laden but scarcely disguised repugnance toward their illnesses. Unlike Kate Brown, who is at first all things to all people, Jane Somers—except in her role as a successful magazine editor—is at first nothing to anybody but Jane Somers.

Her unloving treatment of her two loved ones and her failed effort to compensate afterward by befriending the elderly Mrs. York (11) constitute Jane's false starts on the way to true *reifung*. These false starts bring self-knowledge, the desire to change her self and take charge of her life—salient elements of the *Reifungsroman*. Jane summarizes in the first seven pages four years of false starts without the use of dialogue in halting, disjointed, self-critical language that reflects her groping toward honest self-analysis and analysis of her family relationships ("Yet we could not talk to each other. Correction. Did not talk . . . Correction. He could not talk to me because . . . I shied away" 6). She informs readers that through these false starts she has learned that she is not a nice person: she is selfish, interpreting her husband's and mother's deaths as "unfair" to herself, infecting her with mortality; she is childishly dependent in her private life, "flimsy," in need of "some sort of weight or anchor" (10); she fears intimacy and love. Yet this ironically intimate diary format, which favors the teller and her claims, counteracts the negative self-portrait that Jane gives; despite her litany of repellent traits, we are disarmed by her candor, then start to like her for the small overtures she makes toward Maudie, and finally applaud her for her increasingly generous and courageous kindnesses toward Maudie.

We know that Jane is making a journey of self-discovery and preparation for her future, the typical pattern of the *Reifungsroman*, when at the beginning of the "diary" she says: "Meanwhile I was *thinking* about how I ought to live" (9). She searches for a way to live through her recollections and analysis of her past. Like Kate Brown, she reviews her marriage—a common motif of the heroine, especially the widowed heroine, in *Reifungsromane*—but she reveals her different priorities in one passage by giving her marriage three short sentences (78) after four pages of history on her career. She remembers the good sexual relationship in their marriage (78, 198)—"remembrances of sex past" are also a prominent motif and means of self-affirmation for heroines of most *Reifungsromane*—and longs for Freddie to make love to her again. Yet she gradually realizes that they never talked and that is what she now wishes they had done: "I lie awake sometimes, and what I want is, not that he should be there to make love to me, though I miss that dreadfully, I want to talk to him. Why didn't I talk to him while he was there?" (62). The regret, shared by other heroines of *Reifungsromane* such as Hagar Shipley, is evident in the plaintive tone of Jane's question. Such realizations and rearranging of her priorities prepare Jane for future relationships and enable her eventually to like herself more.

Becoming the daughter-caretaker-nurturing mother of Maudie is another of Jane's vehicles to self-knowledge and self-respect. Jane's relationship with Maudie, she acknowledges, is " 'the one real thing that has happened to me' " (135). Her determination to make this relationship work is evident when she says, "I am a friend . . . of Maudie's only because it was something I decided to do. . . . If you undertake to do something, then it is not absurd, at least to you" (221). This woman speaks out of a new kindness and self-approval; no longer fearful of death or repelled by the old, Jane unites with Maudie, discounting the significance of age.

In befriending Maudie, bathing her, feeding her, cleaning up after her in her final illness, and listening to stories of her past, Jane atones for her failures with her mother and husband and alleviates the shame she feels. Because Jane records her thoughts about what she does in the "privacy" of her diary, readers understand the enormous emotional demands of Jane's undertaking. Jane's ambivalence about Maudie's dependency on her is evident, as is her rationalizing and guilt when she is angry at Maudie. She is horrified at Maudie's condition, yet she forces herself to describe it minutely in her diary as a discipline. Her diary reveals her courage in unflinchingly tackling the grime of Maudie's home and the excrement on her clothing. Although Jane is so repelled at first by her contact with death and old age that she must soak in a tub for hours after visiting Maudie to reestablish her distance from age and to rejuvenate herself (113), gradually the baths become more perfunctory (73), she forgets the dirt, and she acknowledges the rejuvenating bonds between middle age and senescence as she listens to Maudie's tales. Jane hails Maudie's growing trust in her, accepts her dependency. Finally, without panicking at the intimacy between them, she understands Maudie's feeling that these are the best years of her life, that "she [Maudie] is happy now, *because of me*" (88, 126).

That Jane is changing is evident in an extraordinary passage of the diary that Jane writes as if she were Maudie recording a day in her life; Jane clearly wants to empathize with Maudie, to leave behind the egocentric Jane: "I wrote Maudie's day because I want to understand, I *do* understand a lot more about her" (126). To be 49 years old and become 90 years old in mind suggests the invalidity of the polarity Anglo-American culture assumes between youth and age. Jane's "Maudie" passage captures Maudie's bodily ordeals, the strategy to outwit weakness and tiredness (115), the effort of will to move, as revealed in the repetition of words of self-encouragement ("I have to feed the cat, I have to . . . I have to" 115). The passage also evokes the lonely old woman's longing for Jane's visits in a recurring refrain, "Janna will come." And fragmented sentences suggest Maudie's broken thoughts, her mental drifting from sleep to flashbacks to her youth to fantasies of Jane's moving into her apartment. Knowing Maudie by writing her teaches Jane to name the old woman within herself and to live more fully: "I could learn real slow full enjoyment from the very old, who sit on a bench and watch people passing, watch a leaf balancing on the kerb's edge" (166). Indeed, the rhythms of Jane's prose become more leisurely, painstaking, and poetic as she learns. Poetically she feels and writes Maudie's pleasure in the park: "This hot brightly coloured sunlit world was like a gorgeous present" (113).

Learning how Maudie thinks inspires Jane to expand her life in two additional ways: first, to take time away from her magazine and have the "fun" of writing an historical novel, for which "it was Maudie gave me the idea" (123); second, to accept the emotional commitment of taking her niece Jill into her home. Jane thus connects with an elder and a younger woman, even brings Jill to meet Maudie (138–39), and the trio represent age as a continuum, challenging the polarity between youth and senescence.

Jane also breaks down the dichotomy between youth and age when a back ailment invalids her for two weeks, during which she learns, like Kate Brown in her illness, the panicky helplessness of many elders: "For two weeks, I was exactly like Maudie, exactly like all these old people, anxiously, obsessively wondering, am I going to hold out" (131). She uses the same words as Maudie to describe her bodily ills: *"terrible, terrible, terrible!"* (133). Recovered, Jane appreciates her health and independence, decides to decrease her working hours at the magazine and enjoy herself in midlife, and works out a compromise between her former fastidiousness of toilette and the "tired slovenliness" that is "the trap of old age" (217). Like Kate Brown, although less interested in shedding all her sexuality than in rescuing herself from an overly zealous self-polishing routine, Jane assesses her appearance in the omnipresent mirror of the *Reifungsroman* (124), acknowledges that the younger Jane's grooming rituals have become too demanding (127), rejects the expensively detailed, yet understated style she has been known for and can describe so precisely ("My style is that at first people don't notice, and then their eyes come back and they examine detail, detail, the stitching on a collar, a row of pearl buttons" 65), and simplifies her rituals to reflect changes in her priorities and her psyche, including her naming of the old woman within herself.

Jane's language also becomes simpler, more direct. She can tell her loquacious neighbor Mrs. Penny to leave: " 'I must rest now' " (135). She can urge her colleague Joyce to talk to her about her marital problems and confront them. She can bluntly persuade Maudie to take her medicine: " 'It could be a question of your dying before you have to' " (137). That her language is now closer to her feelings indicates that Jane bravely owns these feelings.

Perhaps most noteworthy is the change in Jane's attitude toward old age's companion, death. Attending Maudie in the hospital, Jane can finally observe, "my general air . . . belongs to those who are not upset by dying, death"; and "Once I was so afraid of old age, of death, that I refused to let myself see old people in the streets. . . . Now I . . . watch and marvel" (220; 237). At the end of this *Reifungsroman*, Jane is more receptive to relationships with old people, freed from a debasing fear of old age and death that she had associated with elders, and freed to permit herself more fun *because* death is at the end of life.

Some of the psychic changes inchoate in Jane at the end of *The Diary of a Good Neighbor* are more fully manifested in the sequel, *If The Old Could* . . . (1984). Jane continues to acquire knowledge of herself, seeking answers to such basic questions as "On whom did I model myself?" (264), learning more about the ageless need to be loved and the varieties of love, and expanding her capacity to love.

In this sequel, a more loving Jane also continues to reject self-absorption and cowardice about death by reaching out to the elderly Annie Reeve. Although she never achieves the intensity of love with Annie that she had felt for Maudie, Jane visits Annie regularly and listens to her raging about others' abandonment of her: "it is those who visit the old . . . often and regularly who get shouted at and abused. . . . I can judge the degree of intimacy I have achieved with Annie by how much she grumbles, accuses, rages" (313). As in *The Diary of a Good Neighbor*, Jane writes an entry from the point of view of this lonely and bored old woman (414–23), projecting how the endless hours of the day stretch before her; this imagery of dragging time appears in many *Reifungsromane*. Jane uses the repetitious phrase "watching and watching and watching" to suggest how Annie keeps observing the hands of her clock slowly moving while the contrasting flurry of others' scheduled activities continuously occurs around her (416–17). Her isolation and frustrated craving to chat with rushed caregivers are also noted. Through this interior view, readers can sympathize with Annie's "protesting about time itself, the deceiver, who has whisked her life away from under her feet" (424). Jane's empathy with Annie is clear in her writing of the entry. While Jane recognizes that for many " 'The very old are too frightening, too much of a threat, . . . *mementoes mori*' " (346), she enjoys connecting with the old through writing and visiting, insisting on what she wryly calls her "eccentric" notion that death is not fearful (408). Jane vows not to face her own death as if it were the arch-enemy (426). As she holds the dying Annie's hand, readers cannot help but contrast this Jane to the Jane who fearfully and guiltily avoided her dying husband and mother.

Not only does Jane again reach out to the old in this novel, but also to the young; this time, however, the outreach is much more challenging. Whereas in *Good Neighbor*, Jane extended her helping hand to her competent and attractive niece Jill, who modeled herself after her Aunt Jane and became almost a parodic double (she "really is my younger self . . . she became me, put on my characteristics" 263), in this novel Jane tries to help two troubled, withdrawn young women who are very different from herself. Jane's success in helping Jill's younger sister Kate, the slovenly, unhappy, directionless member of the family, is limited, and seems initially a false start or failure on the road to maturity and integrity characteristic of the heroine of the *Reifungsroman*.

Niece Kate wallows in infantile inactivity and food binges while she puts off thoughts about her future. Jane is clearly repelled by her as she describes Kate's consumption of a package of sliced ham: "Kate . . . started cramming it in. . . . A half-pound of ham disappeared in a moment; she wiped her pudgy grubby hand across her mouth and burped" (427). Jane's challenge is to civilize this primitive, unpleasant girl. Kate is as far from Lessing's Kate Brown as the writer can make her; again there is the suggestion of a parody of the earlier novel in this novel's Kate.

Kate also seems to be the very opposite of her aunt—or is she? Jane's defensiveness concerning her niece is suspect, even as Jane tries to help her. As with Annie, Jane writes a portion of the narrative from Kate's point of view, "A Day in the Life of a Derelict Girl" (363–70), in order to understand Kate better. The girl's fear of Jane's disapproval, resentful dependence on Jane (similar to an elder's dependence), fantasies of success, and hostile withdrawal into a world of rock music and junk food are all expressed here. Jane shows keen intuition in these diary entries' glimpses into Kate and Annie's inner lives. Together they create a discourse that eases the cultural tensions between youth and age and also offers what feminist theorist Jean Bethke Elshtain describes as "a compelling account of human subjectivity and identity" (142). For Jane, however, creating this age-transcending discourse is not without pain. She acknowledges how frustrating is her search for a language she can use to help Kate: "The words for her are some I cannot even imagine . . . somewhere inside me I must be convinced that the words exist which will reach Kate. I have only to find them!" (430). Moreover, her alternating revulsion and affection for Kate run so high that they seem threatening to Jane's concept of herself. Perhaps she is a painful reminder of what Jane might have become had she modeled herself after someone else. Jane confesses, "I begin to see that dull pain which is what . . . Kate demands of me as a symptom of inadequacy: mine" (304). Jane analyzes herself: maybe the Jane whose brisk competence intimidates Kate was once like Kate, a sloppy, lost waif for whom efficiency was not easy, so she had to overdo it (436–37). She learns through Kate's reaction to her that she may not be immaculate, competent Jane by nature, but by a strenuous effort. Through her relationship with Kate, she reviews her youthful self, seeking answers to questions about her identity: "What was I really like as a girl, before I came to London . . .? Was I like Kate . . .?" (437). In fact, the number of sentences framed as questions grows as Jane's search for herself intensifies.

In middle age, then, Jane, like Kate Brown, is searching for an understanding of who she was and is, so she can decide whom she

wants to become—not the stereotype of middle age as complacency and sluggishness. While Jane at first associates middle age
with stagnation, comparing it, as Kate Brown does, to midsummer
("July [is] the year's middle age, when nothing much happens for
what seems like for ever, only insidious intimations of the changes
to come" 370), she at the same time anticipates change in middle
age and readies herself for it by opening her heart to Kate. Although
she is unable to pull Kate out of her unhappiness and give her a
direction in life, Jane does support her while she drifts, and Kate
eventually takes charge of her own life. Moreover, her "failure"
with Kate has taught Jane much about herself. She has also learned
about the nature of interactions between youth and age, as expressed in a passage where she compares a photo of herself at age
23 to her reflection in the inevitable mirror of the *Reifungsroman*:
"I saw . . . me as I must seem to Kate. The unreachable accom-
plishment of it, this woman standing there so firm on the pile of
her energetic and successful years. What a challenge, what a
burden, the middle-aged, the elderly, are to the young" (286). Here
Jane acknowledges both her age and her intimidating impact on
youth. She sees from several chronological perspectives—the truly
" 'Jane'us-headed" middle-ager—challenging the dualistic view
of youth versus age through her understanding of all ages.

Kathleen is the other youth to whom Jane extends herself.
Lessing playfully suggests through the names and the characters'
similar behavior that Kathleen-Kate are doubles, both shadowy
figures, aimless, suicidally unhappy, and haunting their elders as
reminders of their elders' inadequacies. Kathleen trails after her
father, Richard Curtis, the man with whom Jane becomes roman-
tically involved, whenever he has a rendezvous with Jane, just as
Kate follows Jane and hangs about outside her office. Kathleen's
presence severely inhibits the sexually charged interaction between Richard and Jane, which is surely what she wants to do: "Her
being there cancelled everything. . . . Between me and Richard the
current had been cut" (477–78).

Despite Kathleen's inhibiting effect on Jane and Richard's relationship, Jane does not give up on Kathleen. Whereas with Kate

after her suicide attempt, she feels like a failure (495), with Kathleen Jane feels optimism because she represents a continuing link to her father after he and his wife leave England. Her optimism about Kathleen suggests Jane has acquired some "youthful" optimism about life and its opportunities for change, undermining the traditional opposition between quixotic, curious, changeful youth and complacent, jaded, pessimistic middle and old age. Jane expresses this curiosity and sense of adventure to Richard, " 'I wonder what I will be feeling, let's say in a year? . . . Perhaps I'll love her. . . . Why not, when you think of all the jolly little surprises life has in store?' " (500). Although there may be a tinge of seasoned irony about life's surprises in these remarks, Jane's words also indicate that she has rejected her former narrow conservatism about life; now more spontaneous and receptive to change, she gamely travels down new paths in life.

The major new path that Jane travels down in *If the Old Could . . .* is the path of romantic love; in this novel, Jane succeeds in reaching out to the old, to the young, and now to the middle-aged in Dr. Richard Curtis, creating a symbolic unity along the age continuum. That Jane's dormant sexuality is dramatically rekindled in middle age seems, again, a reversal or parody of Kate Brown's redesignation of sexuality as a lower priority in middle age. And Jane finds this reassertion of her sexuality as exhilarating and liberating as Kate finds shedding her sexuality. In both heroines, however, Lessing is still challenging Anglo-American culture's dualities regarding age, especially its tendency to assign sexual activity to youth, not age. The fact that Richard is a doctor, and a doctor whose career has taken second place to that of his wife, a gifted surgeon, also connects this novel parodically to *The Summer Before the Dark*, where Kate Brown was married to a doctor whose career was preeminent; the power positions of the wife and the husband within the two marriages are also exactly reversed.

Pursuing her avocation as a romance novelist helps to open Jane to romantic love in her middle years. Lessing's gentle mockery of the Harlequin romance is apparent in the manner and season in

which Jane and Richard meet: in spring the handsome stranger
Richard catches her in his arms to prevent her from falling (259).
However, the damsel in distress and the handsome stranger of the
Harlequin romance are customarily much younger than Jane and
Richard and much more innocent. Yet Jane still has some learning
and growing to do. By the time they part in September, Jane, the
proper heroine of the *Reifungsroman*, has fully matured, having
for the first time learned about the intense joy and pain of passionate love—in middle age.

In loving Richard, Jane must come to terms with her past failure
to love her husband; review and reassessment of married life are
important aspects of *Reifungsromane*. Jane acknowledges that she
withheld her best self from her husband, channeling her energies
into her work at *Lilith Magazine*. From her work, not from her
marriage, Jane derived most of her life's pleasure: "Doing it well.
That has been my life's theme. And poor Freddie? The background
to it" (281). Now, with Richard in her waking life, Jane dreams
every night that she is making love with Freddie, "full of regret
and longing" for the relationship she had kept in the background
of her life (293). Jane understands now what she was depriving
herself and her husband of in their marriage. She haltingly recon-
structs and analyzes her past, especially her marriage, through her
current dream life, as did Kate Brown, trying to determine whether
or not she ever loved Freddie, toying in wry, self-deprecating
sentence fragments with the word "love" and attempting to redefine and understand it as she reports her dreams: "I dreamed of
Freddie, my lost love. Who was never my love. Or I don't think
he was. It is strange what a bad memory I have for the things that
matter" (311). Clearly Jane's priorities are changing; love is what
matters to her now. Opening up to Richard, discovering the meanings of love and her capacity to love, she attains a clearer perspective on her marriage and her former measured self, whom she now
ruefully characterizes as "that cold girl, negotiating allowances of
emotion, of sex" (277).

Her dreams of Freddie also uncover for Jane her new need to be
loved and to have Richard tell her he loves her, a need our society

usually associates with adolescence. While her mind is still questioning the words, cynically probing into the meaning of love
("Love? *What* love? Love *whom*?" 455), the rest of Jane lies in bed
erotically fantasizing Richard's embrace and whispering of *I love
you*. Readers can hear the longing tone in her confession of passion
as it mingles with her embarrassment about the strength of her
feelings; it seems inconsistent for cool, competent Jane to feel such
passion, and the subtle message from society is that it is inappropriate, "unnatural" for middle-aged people to be swept away by
romantic, erotic love: "With part of myself I was . . . discom-
forted. . . . At the same time my senses were dissolving with the
wanting just that . . . , I love you, I love you. I love you—what
nonsense, like a spell or a drug, the words feeding fevers, the
tongue fattening on the pleasure of saying them" (455). Her
hypnotic repetition of the words builds up for readers Jane's
"adolescent" fever pitch of passion, her intoxication with both
Richard and romantic love. He is not, like Freddie, the background
of her life, but a central focus. Jane makes time away from her
work, bent on seeking pleasure with him. She is girlishly unsettled,
almost swept away by her feelings, belying the stereotypical
portrait of the stolid, complacent, asexual middle-aged woman. In
this novel, much more than in *The Summer Before the Dark*,
Lessing suggests that sexuality is a motivating force all along the
age continuum.

Jane candidly explores her sexual feelings for Richard, writing
the middle-aged woman's body, the language of desire. Without
more than holding her hand, his effect on her body is intensely
erotic, vitalizing, transfiguring, as Jane's biological-alchemical
imagery suggests: "every gland in my body was shooting out
magical substances and . . . my blood must be ichor" (267). Ichor,
the rarified, eternizing fluid of the gods, now runs in her veins. The
heat that the lovers radiate is apparent as they face each other,
"ablaze with love" (267). A rejuvenated Jane enjoys the "outrageous delight" of falling in love at first sight and feels the youth's
restlessness born of her stimulated hormones, "an energy that made
it hard even to sit still" (270). Jane lets herself be taken over by

these pleasurable feelings, permits herself to disregard her pride and loosen her controlled self in order to experience with Richard for the first time in her life an abandonment to gaiety (284).

While she is rejuvenated by this resurgent sexual feeling, Jane at the same time is ironically more aware of her years and the aging of her body. Like Kate Brown, she chooses not to hide those years, but to display them in her graying hair, which she describes in pointedly attractive language, using images of precious metals: "I propose to keep my metallic locks, gold and silver" (266). Yet she also observes that attending to her grooming and clothing is "a holding operation against an invisible enemy who is every day becoming stronger" (268). The martial metaphor suggests that the rapidly advancing invisible enemy, old age, is to be battled or held at bay by subterfuge and strategy (to fool even a lover), but ultimately must be surrendered to on a day of shame. This language suggests that Jane still grapples with her culture's assumption that the young, not the old, are entitled to love and that sexuality is natural for the young, not the old; her sexual fantasies have in them a tone of regret that she is beyond youth: "If I were with Richard, and *young*—I would wait for him to unbutton, slide sensuous stuffs off flesh, *take possession*" (278). The fantasy paints her as a young woman capable of enticing a man, even though she did not in youth feel this sensuality and desire to be possessed sexually. She is experiencing the philosophical and situational irony of the French proverb that is the novel's epigraph and also gives the novel its title: "If the young knew . . . /If the old could . . ." The proverb's dualistic implication is that the young, while possessing the attractiveness, energy, and wherewithal, lack the knowledge of life and love to employ those qualities successfully, while the old have acquired the crucial knowledge, but have lost the attractiveness and wherewithal to use the fruits of that knowledge. The old dualities survive here, although Jane elsewhere synthesizes the youth's attractiveness and energy with the elder's knowledge in her relationship with Richard.

More graphically illustrating the novel's dualistic epigraph is the scene mentioned earlier in which Jane recognizes the burdens that age (Jane) places on youth (niece Kate) when she juxtaposes a youthful photo of herself to her reflection in the mirror. As she appraises herself in the mirror, Jane squarely confronts the aging process, sees the changes in herself: "the girl in the little photograph is so strong an assault on the senses, all dew and juices. . . . And now, here is this solid woman with no light in her, no grace. It is all achieved, done for" (285). Light, naturalness, dew, juices—imagery of sensuous, fertile youth—imply the opposite for age: darkness, artifice, aridity, sterility. The ichor coursing through her veins has evaporated. On another occasion she observes herself naked in front of the mirror, without the achieved effects, the camouflage of clothing, and realizes she has been rationalizing away her own aging: "Oh, I certainly have been deluding myself. Not much changed, I've been thinking vaguely, adjusting over my ageing body the clever clothes I wear" (293). Lessing, through Jane and a mirror, is vividly "writing the body" of the middle-aged woman, making readers scan the text like middle-aged women, so that they mourn the loss of youthful elasticity in Jane's flesh as if it were their own. Readers thus understand why to bring this middle-aged, desiccated, artificially attractive flesh to bed with Richard depresses Jane: "When I do think . . . about making love with Richard, woe invades me, an emptiness, as if I were proposing to bring a ghost to a feast" (293). She would be bringing the ghost of her youthful body, the shadow of her former self, to this love feast, and Jane is mortified by her dry offering to Richard.

This self-consciousness concerning the aging body in love, instead of thwarting Jane's sexual impulses, prompts Jane to keep the sexual intensity, but redefine sexual satisfaction as a "closeness . . . [that is] warm, intimate, with the friendliness of sensuality" (326). With a new philosophical wisdom, Jane questions her society's "must have" view of sexual intercourse: "Why is it we have made an imperative of sex?" (326). She denies the necessity for sexual consummation in her relationship with Richard, finds their electrical interactions intoxicating without it. To have sexual relations, even to kiss, might detract from the eroticism of their relationship: "Passion, . . . it is all there, imminent, incipient, like a country . . . that some mysterious law forbids us to enter. . . . If our lips did meet . . . something would at that moment die" (401). What would die is the delicious anticipation of pleasure in the unknown countries of their bodies, the erotic fantasies that precede consummation.

Jane and Richard find the absence of sexual activity liberating in another way too. They gradually see all the burdensome psychological baggage of the past that older people bring to a new relationship, that they must take to bed with them. This baggage of the past is the interfering ghost that would really haunt their love feast. When Richard visits Jane's flat and sees her bed, both fantasize about making love there, but Richard articulates the question in both of their minds, " 'If all the lights were off, Janna—but then, who would we be making love with?' " (310). At least two other people would be in bed with them, Freddie and Richard's wife Sylvia. Richard's children, as well as Jane's obligations to her nieces, would also help to short-circuit the electricity between them. This baggage from the past represents an undeniable difference between a union of the young and one of the old, as Jane observes to Richard: " 'When a young person gets married, there's not much to them. . . . But people of our age, it's like two continents in collision' " (347). People of middle age have complex histories and networks of demanding relationships, which Jane calls "continents." Jane and Richard decide to avert global conflicts by sustaining a nonsexual, but not asexual, relationship that still affords them considerable pleasure. Lessing has invented an eroticism of the old comparable in intensity and pleasure to the eroticism of the young.

When Jane and Richard part after the summer, Jane is a richer, wiser, more compassionate, and more sensual woman. Although she sheds many tears over the sundering of this "marriage of true minds" (Richard's words, 498), she feels more capable of shaping her future because she has been touched by love. While she must finally confess that her life "is nothing, nothing at all, and never has been" (501), she also recognizes that the present is a tabula rasa on which to write her future, even as she has written this diary.

In fact, in the final lines of her diary Jane's writing moves into a new genre, suggesting new challenges to her creativity and a vision of the future filled with hope and positive anticipation. Jane envisions her future as a play about to begin; the metaphor is charged with energy and purpose as she, the playwright, director, and actor, imagines: "A stage set! House lights down . . . the sudden hush . . . the curtain goes up . . ." (502). As the syntax of the passage trails off into Jane's future, it suggests that this is no cold, passive old age beckoning menacingly to a heroine paralyzed with trepidation, but instead a suspenseful, wonderful poising on the edge of a new world, and Jane is center stage, youthfully eager for the dramatic action ahead.

Lessing's heroines Jane Somers and Kate Brown challenge their society's dichotomizing of youth and age and reject common assumptions about middle age's complacency, flagging powers, and stagnation. Lessing teaches that middle age is a time for reassessing one's personal history, rediscovering one's selves, making exhilarating changes in one's life, and reordering priorities to make a more intense, pleasurable, and significant old age possible. In middle age, personal authenticity is established, safe-guarded, cherished. The personal histories of Kate Brown and Jane Somers also suggest that middle-aged women acquire a maturer, more confident philosophical wisdom, and an iconoclasm that prompt them to question prevailing cultural notions about sexuality, love, marriage, and death; women learn to identify and redefine the concepts and needs that are basic to their existence. In Lessing's *Reifungsromane*, women truly grow up, truly acquire self-mastery, or as Susan Rubin Suleiman has said, truly "assume . . . [their] own subjecthood" (7). Lessing's fiction reminds readers that although the elasticity and juices of youth may diminish, a great deal takes their place in the years between 40 and 60.

ALICE ADAMS'S MIDDLE-AGED
WOMEN-ADVENTURERS

With good reason the short stories of American writer Alice Adams have appeared regularly in the prestigious annual O. Henry Award Collections. Robert Michael Green describes her gifted writing: "At its best, Alice Adams's reportorial style reminds us of Saroyan, Katherine Mansfield, and Hemingway's most innocent (and charming) stories. That's good company." Adams's concern in her fiction with the experiences of aging and emotions of middle-aged women also puts her in the company of Doris Lessing; her middle-aged heroines, like Lessing's, travel on psychic journeys to themselves, "ripening" or acquiring the greater maturity and wisdom that characterize women of *Reifungsromane*. During the 1970's—when *The Summer Before the Dark* was published—and into the early 1980's, Adams wrote a series of short story gems that were collected, titled *To See You Again*, and published in 1982. Several of the stories in the collection are *Reifungsromane* in miniature, and three that depict middle-aged women, "Lost Luggage," "A Wonderful Woman," and the title story, "To See You Again" enable readers to experience middle age intensely.

To Adams, middle age for women is often synonymous not with complacency and boredom, but with upheaval in longstanding relationships and with the brave formation of new relationships; Phyllis L. Thorn has observed that Adams "writes especially well of people in their middle years whose marriages have come apart through divorce or death, . . . whose new 'relationships' are tentative and frightening as well as loving, rich, and rewarding." Thorn's words aptly describe the situation of the heroines in these three stories. The first two depict middle-aged widows embarking on literal and psychic journeys that promise adventure and self-discovery, a typical pattern in *Reifungsromane*. Benjamin De Mott has hailed this fictional widow-adventurer as the "new-style picaresque heroine" and notes that in depicting such heroines, Adams is able to explore "the feelings and impulses . . . [that] lie close to the core of contemporary emotional life" (7). The third story gives us a portrait of a woman not literally but virtually widowed through the mental illness of her husband. She embarks on her journey of self-discovery not by traveling but by taking a job, during which she develops a crush on a young man. In the first two stories especially, the two women start out anxious about the experiences they are to have, but emerge sounder for them, more self-confident and self-knowledgeable. The third story's protagonist has only an internal journey, a set of fantasies reminiscent of Kate Brown's and Jane Somers's rich inner lives. Yet she, like Adams's other two heroines, also changes, becoming more optimistic about her old age, even if middle age's obstacles to happiness seem formidable to her. As De Mott wryly observes, "Readers in north central middle age will doubtless be heartened . . . by the lively desire and splendid resiliency of this author's senior citizen-changelings" (7). De Mott's tinge of flippancy here probably reflects his own uncomfortable, stereotypical thoughts about aging. He fails to give Adams credit for creating appealing, courageous middle-aged heroines who have the power to change not only themselves, but also readers' common notions of middle age for women.

Felicia Lord is the "wonderful woman" of that ironically titled story. The irony of the title is that while everyone considers her a wonderful woman who copes admirably with the death of her husband and other major difficulties, Felicia disparages her own conduct, insisting she has not acted out of choice or strength of character: "Wonderful is not how Felicia sees herself at all; she feels that she has always acted out of simple—or sometimes less simple—necessity" (125). There is a clear discrepancy between the way she perceives herself and the way others perceive her, especially as the narrator encourages readers to see Felicia in attractive terms, with positive observations filling the opening paragraphs; she is pretty, a "stylish gray-blonde," and strong, a "survivor" of marriage to an alcoholic artist manqué (now dead) and five children (now grown) and of a love affair with a Mexican man, ending in an abortion. In short, she is a determined, complex, active woman whose creative yet unpretentious bent is summed up when the narrator describes her as "a ceramicist who prefers to call herself a potter" (123). Felicia's self-disparagements, conveyed through third-person limited omniscient narration, seem misplaced beside such praise. The narrator does not directly explain the discrepancy between internal and external assessments of Felicia, an omission that, as Elizabeth Forsythe Hailey has suggested, is typical of Adams's reportorial style: "Writing in a deliberately flat style, she refuses to tell you what she expects you to discover for yourself." However, it is clear that Felicia is not accurately or fully acquainted with herself.

In the course of this story Felicia's self-disparagement and ignorance of herself end as she undergoes intensive self-examination while she waits for her lover in a San Francisco hotel. While waiting and wondering whether he will appear for the rendezvous, Felicia, like Kate Brown and Jane Somers, has "remembrances of sex and loves past," a common element of *Reifungsromane*. This scrutiny of her past enables her to acknowledge her strength, her ability to survive alone, and her basic wonderfulness. Like an enthusiastic and idealistic 16-year-old, she feels exhilarated about her new romance; her future seems brimming with possibilities. Yet the opening sentence suggests that like a naïve and vulnerable 16-year-old, she initially fears the failure of this relationship with a man, as she embarks on it "at her age"; her self-deprecating tone in this last phrase is also a reprise of the old attitude that love is for the young and old love is somehow inappropriate. However, reviewing her rich history of romantic attachments allows her to see that she has successfully weathered romantic crises and is equipped either to venture into new love in middle age or to meet her future without a romantic relationship. The traditional borders between the emotional domains of youth and age become blurred in Adams's depiction of Felicia's romantic feelings.

Adams scrutinizes Felicia's panic at the thought that this meeting and this relationship will fail. Self-conscious and insecure in this new "inappropriate" role, Felicia feels less sure of "what she is about" than the bellboy who, she paranoically thinks, smiles knowingly at her (123). The narrator describes her unsettling emotions, her disorientation in this role of lover at age 59, through physical sensations: Felicia feels a "dizzying lurch of apprehension . . . intense in its impact," and "suddenly quite weak," she has to sit down (124). As she looks out the window in her dizzy state, even the rooftops have a "crazy variety," reflecting and increasing her disorientation. Felicia's thoughts leap from crazy roofs to questions about her crazy relationship with Martin, a risky departure from her customary kind of man. This "farming sailor" defies her usual categorizing; Martin is "entirely new to her" (124). Is this, she wonders, an imprudent decision by a formerly wonderful, sensible woman—inappropriately daring for a woman just short of 60? Is this a false start on the road to true *reifung*, such as Kate Brown experienced in her liaison with Jeffrey Merton? And is San Francisco an inappropriate place for this meeting, given its role in her past relationships, the history that she is about to reminisce over? As she waits for Martin, questions and doubts punctuate her inner monologue, mirroring her society's assumptions about youth and age: her romantic feelings and risk taking are deemed embarrassing for one of her "advanced" age. Her fear of failure, then, comes not only from her sense of personal inadequacy, but also from her sense of having overstepped social bounds by reaching for "youthful" pleasures; images of natural catastrophe express her fear of the consequences of this "unnatural" liaison that tampers with nature: "Supposing she isn't 'wonderful' anymore? Suppose it all fails, flesh fails, hearts fail, and everything comes crashing down upon their heads, like an avalanche, or an earthquake?" (126). The doubts that strike her are reminiscent of Jane Somers's dismay as she stands in front of the mirror naked, sees her juiceless body, and fantasizes making love with Richard. Readers increasingly sympathize with Felicia as the waiting period stretches out, sharing her dismay that she may have been abandoned. The doubts, the excitement, the suspense, and a virus combine to make Felicia sick.

Some of Felicia's doubts during this interminable waiting period are eased by the arrival of Martin's telegram informing her that a "crazy delay"—the word "crazy" linking the telegram with the crazy San Francisco roofs and her sense of the craziness of planning such a rendezvous at all—will keep him from her for a few days. The delay enables her to consider whether the liaison itself is crazy, allows her to be sick and convalesce, and gives her time to reexamine her past in order to reassess herself and prepare for her future.

She experiences in abbreviated form (appropriate to the short story) Kate Brown's momentous summer of illness, introspection, and maturation. Felicia reviews her courtship and marriage to Charles and her mothering of their five children, her love affair with Felipe (a false start on the path to maturity), and the recent history of her passion for Martin. As she takes to her bed and reminisces, she feels older, no longer like the romantic 16-year-old for whom the silk and lace lingerie she wears is appropriate, but instead decked out like "an old circus monkey,"—echoing Kate Brown's self-description when ill and aging like a thin, sick monkey. Felicia imagines that the bellboy grins at her with malice and contempt, seeing her as "an abandoned woman, of more than a certain age" (129). She fantasizes her illness spiraling to death and herself becoming "an unknown dead old woman" in this hotel room (129). Old age, illness, helplessness, abandonment, death: she faces squarely in this fantasy some of the grisly myths about senescence, gathering strength to puncture them.

Moreover, as she remembers her past, Felicia demythicizes it. This demythicizing is necessary so that her past will not have the power to thwart newly developing aspects of her future. First she remembers her fairytale courtship with her husband during the glamour of wartime: brief leaves, dancing all night in elegant hotels, the marriage proposal during a champagne breakfast; Adams selects the concrete details of the reminiscence carefully to suggest its romanticized quality in Felicia's mind. Then Felicia, like Jane Somers, confronts the real emptiness of her marriage, her lack of love for her dead husband; "having seen the lonely, hollow space behind his thin but brilliant surface of good looks, graceful manners," Felicia remembers feeling so sorry for this despairing failed artist that "it was then impossible to leave him" (125).

Similarly, Kate Brown contemplates her husband's weakness for affairs with younger women and recognizes the flaws in their marriage. For Kate, Jane, and Felicia, the starry-eyed view of marriage is gone. Felicia dismisses one of her youthful illusions, "a dream of a courtship, and then a dream groom" (127).

As part of her assessment of her marriage, Felicia, like Kate Brown, also scrutinizes her role as a mother. She does not see herself as a good mother, not having liked young children, and is grateful that she has gone beyond the role so that she can see her grown children "with great fondness, and some distance" (128). Unlike Kate, Felicia experiences no empty nest syndrome. She simply dismisses another of her life's myths, that of her being the devoted mother of five. Again she is confronted by the undeniable flatness of her married life: if children are at the center of their marriage and Charles married her mainly to be the mother of his children, she has not discharged her maternal role so "wonderfully" (128).

Felicia also reexamines her "ideal" romantic relationship with her Mexican Communist artist-lover Felipe, whose macho, radical style swept Felicia off her feet. Their passionate affair results in her pregnancy, an emotionally agonizing abortion in San Francisco, and, finally, Felipe's return to his wife. Another dream is shattered: a dream of passionate romance: "And she thought, 'Well, so much for my Latin love affair' " (131). She is gradually realizing how well she has survived, summoning strength, courage, and the will to go on. Phyllis L. Thorn observes this resilience in many of Adams's female characters: they are "courageous and resourceful people with an appealing talent for starting over and making new beginnings." As she reexamines her history and learns to appreciate her own emotional stamina, Felicia is also convalescing from her physical illness. Her physical recovery reinforces the idea that she is becoming more self-knowledgeable and more self-congratulatory.

The most challenging aspect of Felicia's reminiscence concerns the new history of her relationship with Martin, whom she has known for only a few months. It is too soon to know and trust him, she realizes, yet here she is in San Francisco waiting to meet him. He has asked her to marry him, a proposition that she knows requires mutual trust, but now she ironically doubts whether he will even show up at the hotel. Finally she faces the possibility of a future without him. It may hurt at first, "the possible loss of such a rare, eccentric and infinitely valuable man" (131), but with her history to buttress her, Felicia "realizes that she can stand it, after all, as she has stood other losses, other sorrows in her life. She can live without Martin" (132). Felicia reaches this conclusion out of conviction; she realizes that she is not just whistling in the dark after having reviewed her painful history and track record of survival. She can live alone comfortably. And readers nod approvingly as she goes out to a nice dinner by herself, acknowledging that to dine alone is "really not so bad" (132). However, feelings of weakness and childishness return when, back at the hotel, she is disappointed that Martin has still not arrived.

Like Lessing, Adams uses a dream to explore further Felicia's conflicts and ambivalence about her newly acknowledged autonomy; dreams are central to the heroine's self-examination in most *Reifungsromane*. She dreams a man comes to her room at night and although thrilled to see him, she is not sure who he is: "Is it her husband Charles, or one of her sons? Felipe? Is it Martin? It could even be a man she doesn't know" (132–33). She confesses that the dream saddens her, perhaps because in it she is so happy to see the man, suggesting that despite her struggle for autonomy, she is dependent on men for happiness, after all; or she may be saddened because in the dream Martin is identified with the other men in her life with whom her relationships turned out to be disappointing or limited. Her ambivalence about solitude versus male companionship is evident in either interpretation of the dream.

This ambivalence in her dream life is overtaken by Felicia's increasing enjoyment of her own companionship during her waking hours. She appraises herself in the omnipresent mirror of the *Reifungsroman* and sees, more optimistically than Jane Somers, "a strong healthy older woman" (133). She no longer waits passively

in her hotel room for her lover, but tours San Francisco, pleased
by her own company. By the time Martin arrives, Felicia has
matured by facing her past, becoming comfortable with her present
aloneness, and recognizing her own strength for the future.

Martin's arrival in the middle of the night is like her dream: she
cannot at first identify who he is. When she does, she is glad to see
him. Yet she has learned that her future is not contingent solely
upon him or this relationship. Regardless of what may happen in
her relationship with Martin, Felicia ends her story confident that
she will again be a survivor—finally giving herself credit for being
one—a survivor with many options before her. Felicia Lord acknowledges herself "lord" of her own destiny. By empowering
Felicia in this way, Adams is no longer giving credence to American society's dualistic notion of youth as an epoch of power and
choice and middle age as a time of increasing disenfranchisement
and dependency, particularly for women.

Janet Stone Halloran could be Felicia Lord's sister. The protagonist of "Lost Luggage" describes in a first-person narrative some
of the same experiences and thoughts that Felicia has, although she
appears to be more self-confident at the beginning of her story than
Felicia. Like Felicia, Janet is middle-aged and recently widowed.
When the story opens, she has just returned from her first vacation
alone, for which she congratulates herself with "more than usual
self-approval; you could call it pride or maybe hubris, even" (93).
She has enjoyed her own companionship, socialized with other
people, successfully negotiated the practical details of traveling.
She seems to have adjusted to her middle age, as indicated by her
pleasure in her appearance: "I was brown and silver, like a weathering country house, and I did not mind the thought of myself as
aging wood" (93). Janet counters the stereotyped images of deterioration, gray hair, increasing wrinkles, and sagging flesh with
these lovely images of physical aging as ripening or enhancing
one's appearance. Adams has also written positively about her own
middle age and gray hair in an autobiographical sketch for *Vogue*,
"On Turning Fifty": "My fifties . . . are the best years of my life,

so far . . . and . . . given the proper lighting and a sympathetic photographer, grey hair has a wonderful sheen" (232).

Janet's positive mental outlook initially prevents her from becoming upset over the airline's loss of her suitcase. As the story unfolds, however, she has an emotional relapse triggered by the lost suitcase, a crisis that she has to resolve and whose resolution strengthens her for her future alone. In describing her crisis to the reader, Janet's narrative travels back and forth between her past marriage to Walter and his death, her recent past at the Mexican resort, her present in her San Francisco home, and her future hopes and schemes. The familiar pattern in the *Reifungsroman* of the flashback or reminiscence to analyze and reassess an important marital or sexual relationship from the past before building a new life, present in Felicia Lord's, Kate Brown's and Jane Somers's stories, is central to this story too.

In a sense, as she confronts her literally lost luggage in her present, Janet is also reexamining, in most cases to jettison, the figurative baggage from her past life: her formerly important relationships, values, priorities, even her traditional methods of meaning making in language. Jettisoning as a practice of the middle-aged is explored in articles on aging in popular magazines, but Adams's heroine practices it uniquely in her use of language. To rethink and dislodge meanings stereotypically associated with terms like "gray hair," "widow," "older woman," and "woman alone" frees her language to acquire new meanings, frees her to create new associations for these terms. Kate Brown freed her language during her "cow sessions." Janet's analytic method of sifting through her past and redefining her life is also patently linguistic; she writes her analyses in a large daybook or journal, like Jane Somers and Caro Spencer. Janet's journal is the one item that she really misses in her lost suitcase, until she realizes that what it contained, its meanings, or any meaning need not depend upon what is actually carried, preserved in writing, or handed down, as if in one sacred vessel, one compendious, universal, canonical volume. She realizes that because it is a process, not a "thing," meaning can be continually recreated, reconceptualized, and particularized. This realization prompts Janet's decision to buy not the duplicate of the lost daybook, but the first of several smaller, more portable and more "losable" journals and to fill the first one with new impressions of her Mexican vacation and her life; she will not attempt to reconstruct the original lost jottings. Like Janet in her journals, Adams in this story also creates new meanings for widowhood and middle age.

As she reminisces about her courtship and marriage to Walter, Janet acknowledges what none of her friends had known because Janet is a reserved person. She establishes an intimate tie with the reader by confessing to a failure of love in her marriage, only a lack of money having prevented divorce. They had married "for love (well, sex, really)" (94), but the mutual attraction had faded and left Janet a lonely woman who read obsessively while Walter indulged a penchant for owning expensive cars. She recalls her lack of sympathy for Walter and his hobby with some guilt because of his early death. Guilt is a major item of Janet's baggage from the past that she has to deal with now. In addition, her recollection of their last vacation together at the Mexican resort reveals much about the emptiness of their relationship and about her former conventional attitude toward aging. During their last vacation, both had experienced "a miasma of incommunicable depression" (97) whose source, she determines, was the thought of their aging together, growing apart and deteriorating: "Our slowing middle-aged flesh seemed to parody its former eager, quick incarnation. . . . Is the rest of our life together, if we stay together, to be such a process of attrition?" (97–98). Janet's association of aging with a repellent deterioration acts as a metaphor for the deterioration of their repellent relationship. She conjectures that if one's life is not going well or if it is worsening, aging does not seem to improve it, but merely to mock a person with the contrast to what her life had once been. Without a newly rekindled passion or strengthened identity and purpose to offset its decaying powers, such as Jane Somers, Kate Brown, and Felicia Lord acquire, aging may well become a depressing process of attrition. However, Janet must recognize the deterioration of her relationship with Walter, which aging seemed to aggravate, before she can begin ripening.

At the Mexican resort, Janet records her reminiscences and analyzes them in her daybook; her daybook also records her observations in the present of the other guests at the resort as well as her fantasies about her future as a single woman. By writing in the journal, she can move beyond the initial tendency of the newly widowed to whitewash or idealize the marriage, "to remember . . . [only] the good times between us" (96), so that by the end of her vacation her perspective has become wider and more accurate: "I could remember the good days quite as easily as the bad" (98). She acquires an honest appreciation of Walter and their limited marriage and can even feel the injustice of his early death. She also discovers the important role of writing in her daybook to widen her perspective on her marriage and Walter's death and to chart her progress in mourning and adjusting to widowhood. She emphasizes her preoccupation with the effects of writing on herself by mentioning how moved she had been by Doris Lessing's protagonist Anna and her efforts to understand her life through her scrupulous journal keeping in *The Golden Notebook* (99). Janet also refers readers to passages in her own journal that, when compared, illustrate her progress, beginning with an early nightmarish scene after Walter's death in which she records her viewing of Walter's body in the funeral home and ending with her calmer reflections about her present and her enthusiastic hopes for her future. Unlike the "process of attrition" she had foreseen in her relationship with Walter alive (98), she is as a widow now able, in part through therapeutically writing in her journal, to trace the healing return "to my old self, competent and strong" (100) and to foster new self-growth.

With this strong self as a foundation, Janet assumes a "youthful" outlook toward the future, envisions herself "turning [her] life around": "I would experience an exhilarating sense of adventure . . . I could even, I imagined, find a big house to share with some other working women, about my age—not exactly a commune but a cooperative venture. Such prospects excited and to a degree sustained me" (97). Middle-aged Janet confidently imagines herself as a single working woman, a role that blurs the borders between youth and age by invoking images of smart young *Mademoiselle* businesswomen; and the borders are further blurred by her reference to the commune, youth's challenge to the nuclear family. She does not fantasize about the presence of a man in her future, deciding after observing the conduct of another older single woman at the Mexican resort that the old woman she wants to become is not one who talks too much as if to compensate for not being part of a twosome, or one who buys the company of younger men by paying for their drinks. She will enjoy her singleness, like Felicia.

Because Janet gives the reader much evidence to believe in her new strength, independence, and optimism, the reader is jolted by her severe panic when, back in San Francisco, she realizes her daybook is in her missing suitcase and she may never see it again. She uses a dramatic analogy to describe her panic: "I did not see how I could go on with my life. Everything within me sank. It was as though my respirator, whatever essential machine had kept me breathing, was cruelly removed" (100). The panic is a physical assault, like Felicia's dizzying, weakening lurch of apprehension as she considers the possibility that Martin has abandoned her. Neither woman gives herself credit initially for being able to survive without external support. Janet feels these lost jottings are her lifeline, protecting her from emotional collapse.

Yet as Janet finally discovers, after it becomes apparent that the airline will never locate her luggage, the lost jottings are not so important; it is the process of writing her thoughts down, making connections, making meaning, that matters. Writing in the journal is always a happy time for her as she focuses on herself and sifts through recent or distant events to create meaning out of these experiences. Writing enables her to take charge of her own emotional life.

Janet learns the importance of the process of constant recreating, making new meanings in her life that are not dependent upon those meanings she has inherited and preserved, that baggage she has carried. With this realization, she can resolve her crisis: she will buy a new notebook and start to write again. In deciding to replace the large, bulky, expensive journal with a small, compact one for her journey on the open road of her future, middle-aged Janet is jettisoning: she jettisons excess baggage, a bulky journal into which she had thrown some of her bulky, burdensome, no longer relevant feelings, such as guilt about Walter, feelings that she no longer needs to carry with her. Jane Somers and Richard Curtis could have benefited from a similar jettisoning. Janet learns that if she can continue writing—because writing is like living: engaging, experimental, full of risk taking—then what literally happens in her life is almost immaterial. Whatever happens, she will be able to embrace it, absorb it, make sense of it. Writing in her notebook gives Janet dominion over her life.

What the notebook and the process of writing mean for Janet, Adams seems to hope reading the story will mean, vicariously, for readers: an aesthetic, therapeutic experience and analysis of loss, widowhood, and adjustment to a single middle age. That Janet titles the newest chapter in her life, her first entry in her newly purchased journal, "Lost Luggage," the same title that Adams gives her story about Janet, suggests that Adams means us to see this connection between Janet's writing and our reading of Adams's writing.

Janet ends her narrative with a more solidly anchored self-confidence. She had begun her narrative congratulating herself for looking well as a middle-aged widow and for having survived her first vacation alone. She ends it by quietly stating that she will carry her portable notebook with her during any future trips, testifying to the importance of writing in her life and to her new mobility after some midlife jettisoning. But the confidence of her very last words, "even if the book were to be lost, the loss would be minimal" (106), testifies to her realization that the power and freedom of her writing to create new meanings in her life reside not in the daybook or in the words, but in herself. She knows now that her "strong-as-Stone" (Stone is her maiden name) strength and happiness have been self-won. The fact that she cheerfully takes on a part-time job and a paying house guest near the end of the narrative suggests that she is on her way to fulfilling the exhilarating vision she had had in Mexico of her future as an older woman alone. That she is optimistically future-oriented is further suggested by her declaration in the final paragraph: "I don't plan to go back to that particular Mexican resort; I believe that it has served its purpose in my life" (106). This twice-visited resort now becomes a part of Janet's past, a chapter of her life's journal jettisoned by the writer to ready her for new jottings and new travels. With its firmly cheerful futurity and its challenge to conventional ways of making meanings about middle age, "Lost Luggage" justifies critic Norbert Blei's claim that Adams's writing "can change our lives."

Adams's vision of aging is more ambivalent in the last story of her collection, the title story, "To See You Again." The middle-aged heroine of "To See You Again," Laura, in a first-person narrative reveals how acutely she is aware of her own and other people's ages and the aging process itself. She, like many in American society, sees age as a major constituent of identity, not always with happy consequences. She dislikes herself because she is old in comparison to a 19-year-old man named Seth, with whom she has become infatuated while teaching an English class at Cornford. Advancing age, on the other hand, will diminish her husband's bouts with severe depression, gradually ending her intermittent widowhood. Aging may also improve her interactions with Seth, decreasing the social disparity between their ages. Although Laura experiences despair partly because of her age, by the end of her story she nevertheless imagines a better future in which the burdens of her middle age will be lightened by her entry into old age.

Laura divides her first-person narrative into four segments: one concerning Seth and her feelings for him, representing her false start on her journey to true *reifung*; a second concerning an older male friend, Larry Montgomery; the third concerning her husband Gerald, with the *Reifungsroman*'s familiar reminiscence of courtship and review of marriage; and the fourth concerning a fantasy she has about her future with Gerald and Seth, inspired by a play she sees on television. As she moves through all four segments, she also journeys backward and forward along the age continuum, acquiring a perspective on youth, middle age, and old age.

Laura is more obsessed with the inappropriateness of her feelings for Seth than is Felicia. Felicia merely smiles over her 16-year-old-in-love feelings, unseemly for a 59-year-old woman, but Laura feels it is scandalous and shameful for a middle-aged woman like herself to have a crush on a youth. Her discomfort is evident in her every phrase. She tells us that she is "cruelly older than Seth" (293) and imagines how repelled he must be by her age. She censures herself in the middle of imagining the "act of love" with him; "the very idea [is] both terrifying and embarrassing" because she would be exposing her repulsively middle-aged body to his youthful eyes: "How old I must seem to him! Revolting, really, although I am in very good shape 'for my age.' But to him revolting—as I sometimes am to myself" (295). Laura's words convey her self-loathing, the distaste for her aging flesh that Jane Somers intermittently feels when gazing in the mirror. And Laura does not attain the self-approval in middle age or self-confidence about her old age that Kate Brown and Adams's other two heroines do. She thinks dualistically about aging, and her dualistic imagery reflects her pessimism, as she compares her middle age to the cold of San Francisco, which she then contrasts to Cornford's "adolescent summer—urgent, flushed" (296). Her imagery associates a cold, impassive sterility with middle age while it assigns to adolescence the ripening warmth of insistent sexual passion.

As obsessed as she is with their disparity in age and her aging body, Laura is even more obsessed with the youthful beauty of Seth as she repeatedly describes to us his red-gold curls, green eyes, and bright sensitivity. His beauty seems to increase her own self-loathing as well as her pain at losing him when the semester ends. The barrier between youth and age seems unassailable as the "silly, fatuous" girls, his classmates, literally and metaphorically obstruct her last view of Seth in the classroom; they are her victorious rivals, Seth's peers. Laura tells us that she has put her feelings for Seth in perspective, but her words also suggest that she is still haunted by her feelings for him: "Not quite anguished—I had had worse losses in my life (I have them still)—but considerably worse than 'let down' was how I felt" (294). The only way she can cope with both the age issue and losing him is to fantasize about seeing him in the future, an older, still handsome man, but showing the effects of aging, like herself ("maybe in middle age he will be heavy? I wistfully considered that" 296). No longer a breathtakingly young and beautiful boy, an older Seth would somehow be more "equal" to her, less idealized.

In the second segment of her narrative, Laura's thoughts turn to Larry Montgomery in an effort to understand both how Seth would feel about her if he knew of her infatuation and what she herself would like from Seth: "Larry is exactly as much older than I am as I am older than Seth. He has what Gerald describes as a crush on me" (297). Like Laura herself, Larry is well preserved: "Larry looks at least ten years younger than he is, trim and tan, with lively blue eyes and fine silver-white hair" (297). Through her comparison of the two relationships she learns that she, like Larry, may have at times acted curtly toward the object of her adoration because she was terrified of revealing her affection for him. She also learns that a sexual affair is probably not what either she or Larry would want: "a stray motel afternoon with Larry was as unimaginable as it would be with Seth. Larry just likes to see me, to be near me, sometimes—and very likely that is what I feel for Seth, pretty much?" (297). The question mark at the end of her sentence suggests that Laura is still in the process of analyzing her feelings in order to understand herself; she is not sure what she wants, or could have, from Seth. She imagines herself domesticating her unruly sexual feelings for him, which she so disparages, by making Seth a family friend and inviting him to her home (299). As Laura seeks answers to her questions about Seth, gaining knowledge about her identity and a direction for her future, she is mentally ripening, like most protagonists of *Reifungsromane*.

Important to this ripening process is Laura's probing in the third section of her narrative into her marriage to "sad fat" Gerald, a successful architect who has given her a "most precariously balanced . . . 'good life' " (295). Her marriage to this severely depressed man has been a cold one, and his bouts with depression have undermined Laura's self-approval: "one problem about living with someone who is depressed is that inevitably you think it has to do with you, your fault, although you are told that it is not" (300). That her self-esteem has been eroded by Gerald's illness is evident in her self-demeaning fantasies about the beautiful Seth. Her contrasting of Seth and Gerald only intensifies her despair about herself, her husband, and her marriage. Gerald's fat old man's body and "heavy as boulders" depression (301) contrast with Seth's thin boy's body and sprightly, elfinlike personal qualities. Even the language she uses to describe her home reflects her view of Gerald and their marriage; their kitchen has an atmosphere of "immaculate" sterility, and she, passionate and angry at being deprived of a passional life, imagines herself countering that sterility by painting it red (301).

Following the pattern of *Reifungsromane*, Laura also goes back in her memory to their youth and courtship, which offer another painful contrast to the present. Gerald was then "so beautiful, so dark and thin, . . . so elusive"—qualities of youth that remind us of Seth; and Laura was also young, "a silly undergraduate with a crush on a future architect" (303). The contrast between this past and the present that greets her as she returns home from her final class—Gerald has descended into another depression—dismays her. All that she really has to comfort her is the statement of Gerald's psychiatrist: "With age the cycle [of his bouts with depression] may well lengthen, and the severity of each attack will decrease" (303–4). The psychiatrist's words—like Lessing's and Adams's messages generally—challenge our common association of the aging process with increased depression and despair. That aging may cure Gerald gives Laura something to look forward to, but her question is, will it come soon enough? Laura's words betray her impatience and escalating despair: "age could take forever; I'm not sure I have that much time" (304). The edgy tone of these words implies that she is enduring an unbearable situation and can only continue to do so a little longer. Time is not passing quickly enough—a phenomenon present in *Reifungsromane* about middle age, but even more common to *Reifungsromane* about old age—to cure Gerald, salvage her marriage, and bring Laura some contentment.

To distract herself from the slow passage of time, Laura has only her imagination, which she trains in the fourth section of the story on a television play that she is watching. The play comforts her because in it is an actor who strongly resembles Seth—the obsessed woman sees the face of this youth everywhere—as she imagines he will look in older middle age. She says, "Oh, so that is how he will look: gray, slightly overweight but *strong*, with a brilliant smile, and those eyes" (306). She soothes herself by fantasizing a future meeting with the older Seth, whom she will finally be able to look at because he will have become "merely handsome." Aging has its benefits after all: not only does it cure people of the depression and despair that often assail them in middle age, but it also equalizes people's original endowments of personal beauty. This prospect offered by Laura's fantasy gives her something to look forward to: "And at that time, your prime and our old age, Gerald's and mine, Gerald will be completely well . . . no more sequences of pain. And maybe thin again. And interested, and content. It's almost worth waiting for" (106). What a pretty fantasy, readers think—"and they lived happily ever after," ripening into an old age that is a blessed release from the disappointments and despair of middle age.

But there are two further considerations: one, this is a fantasy that will probably never come true; and two, Laura uses the word "almost": if a perfect fantasy is not completely (as opposed to "almost") worth waiting for, what is? Instead of being a comfort to Laura, this fantasy's contrast to reality may be too painful for her to enjoy or believe in. Perhaps she is not able to wait anymore, meaning her patience and ability to endure her trials have run out in midlife. She may have lost the fight against "disillusionment . . . [and] 'the sheer fatigue of living' " (Gray 80). Because she had said, "age could take forever; I'm not sure I have that much time" to wait for the end to Gerald's illness (304), readers are left at the end of the story with an uneasy feeling about Laura's fragile lease on life, a sense of her inching toward suicide. Old age will be easy for her to embrace, it seems, if she can just make it through a beastly middle age. She has not had the advantages of new love that Jane Somers and Felicia have: their exhilaration and rejuvenation contrast with her despair and shame over her infatuation with Seth; pleasure and happiness seem far removed from Laura's life. Nor does she have the resource of writing in a journal, which improves the tenor and direction of Janet's life. Writing in a journal as a way of coming to terms with the conditions of one's life would be more constructive than escaping from those conditions as Laura does through her fantasies. She seems almost as afflicted by inaction as her clinically depressed husband, achieving no pragmatic resolution of her current problems and foreseeing none in the short run. All is in abeyance till old age. Laura's story ends with her passive resignation to a barely tolerable situation, one that prevents her from garnering the happy fruits of ripening self-knowledge and maturity. In "To See You Again," Adams presents middle age as a time for reassessing one's life and depicts through Laura some likely results of such a reassessment: self-knowledge and ripening maturity, but also confrontation with failures, losses, and disappointments that may be paralyzing, more difficult to bear, and more treacherous than the challenges of old age.

It is curious that Adams chose to end her volume with this story and to give the collection the title of this story. Its ambiguous message about the aging process departs from the unalloyed optimism about middle age in Janet's and Felicia's stories and in other stories of the collection about old age. The story suggests that the period of middle age may be particularly trying and turbulent. And through the story, readers can understand how we torment ourselves on the issue of age—how we denigrate ourselves and others because of the meanings we attach to words like "middle-aged." Perhaps Adams chose to end her book with Laura's story because she is not a whitewasher of reality. That middle age requires some difficult transitions and adjustments to losses is amply attested to also by the struggles of Kate Brown, Jane Somers, Janet, and

Felicia. These transitions and adjustments demand of the protagonists real courage and strength of character. What is, nevertheless,
evident in these fictional heroines is their authors' belief that many
women can develop and unearth rich reserves of courage and
strength within themselves.

3

New Passions and Commitments in Young Old Age

In the past, discussions about the old usually placed them in one chronological category, simply because longevity was not so commonplace that large numbers of people survived past late middle age or early old age. In recent decades, with many people living into their 80's, gerontologists, psychologists, and other observers have begun to see different categories among the elderly, partly based on the condition of health and partly on the kinds of problems and choices faced by people during different transitional phases of their old age. While overlapping of these categories exists, the "young old," aged 60 to 74, frequently face crises and are required to make certain adjustments that the "middle old" (75–85) or the "old old" (over 85) would in all likelihood already have dealt with.

Many authors of *Reifungsromane* recognize these gradations of senescence. They especially like to depict young-old women, a generally healthy and spirited set of women who journey on the high road of life's adventures after a major "liberating" transition in their lives, either from marriage into widowhood, or from work into retirement, or both. Although these major life-style transitions may occur before or after the 60-to-74 years, and although ill health can intervene at any age to alter the life pattern described in this chapter, enough fictional women experience these transitions and exhibit these young-old traits to make some valid generalizations about the young old in contemporary *Reifungsromane*. Many novelists depict in their heroines of this age group an intense emotional turmoil as they adapt to widowhood and retirement. Equally apparent are the strength, flexibility, and ingenuity with which these heroines face major changes in their lives. They do not act "old," in our outmoded sense of the word *old* as being spectators of life. May Sarton distinguishes her young-old outlook from that of old age at the beginning of her journal on her 70th birthday: "I do not feel old at all, not as much a survivor as a person still on her way. I suppose real old age begins when one looks backward rather than forward, but I look forward with joy to the years ahead and especially to the surprises that any day may bring" (9–10).

Novelists Elizabeth Taylor, Barbara Pym, and Paule Marshall are questioning the myth of spectatorship, Golden Pond mellowness, or stagnation in old age as they create *Reifungsromane* in which young-old fictional women with attitudes like Sarton's experience deep passions and take on new, intense commitments to other people, to the preservation of their heritage, or simply to the promises and surprises of the future. Through Taylor's Laura Palfrey, from *Mrs. Palfrey at the Claremont*, Pym's Letty Crowe and Marcia Ivory, from *Quartet in Autumn*, and Marshall's Avey Johnson, from *Praisesong for the Widow*, readers learn how young-old women may become more than mere survivors and onlookers at the game of life.

MRS. PALFREY: A HEARTH OF HER OWN AND A PASSIONATE HEART

When the elderly widow Laura Palfrey—"pale but free" and sturdy as the saddle horse that is her surname—pulls up in a taxi at the Claremont Hotel in London at the opening of Taylor's novel, readers must abandon the stereotype of the old woman knitting peacefully until death at the family's country hearth. Laura Palfrey has purposely chosen to live in London, near all the action: "There was always so much going on in London, she had told her daughter, who had suggested Eastbourne as a more suitable place for her to live. In London there were a great many free entertainments, and a great diversity of people" (8). Mrs. Palfrey wants contact with life's variety, not exclusion from it at some hearth: " 'Peace and quiet are the last things old people want,' " she says. Sounding like a young woman, she later claims, " 'we like to be where something's going on' " (121). To further break down the dichotomy between youth and age and the stereotypical notion of sheltered old age, Taylor's narrator informs us that Mrs. Palfrey is alone and without roots. Through a newspaper advertisement she has discovered the Claremont, which one critic describes as "a halfway house between the homes of their own that its guests once had and the hospitals or nursing homes where they go to die" (Rosenthal 25). The narrator also takes us inside Mrs. Palfrey's mind to reveal that despite a surge of panicky loneliness as she settles into her prison cell of a room at the Claremont, she likes her privacy and would never live in Scotland with her only child Elizabeth, even if such an invitation had ever been forthcoming. It never had because the two are incompatible: her daughter "was noisy and boisterous and spent most of her time either playing golf or talking about it" (21). Thus she has no protective familial hearth, although Mrs. Palfrey is under the delusion that she will have a piece of that hearth with her in her grandson Desmond, who lives and works in London. She fondly (and naïvely) assumes he will visit her often because there is a link between them, " 'a relationship that often skips a generation' " (15). Having this link to the family hearth as well as a "room of her own" suits Mrs. Palfrey. Even so, from the first paragraph Taylor's narrator indicates that Mrs. Palfrey fears and must work to resist depression amidst her new surroundings.

In this room of her own, Mrs. Palfrey experiences the freedom of the old: " 'free of nursery chores and social obligations, one's duty, . . . and free of worries . . . about one's loved ones—. . . the only *way* of being free—to be not needed' " (99). The repetition of the word "free" here becomes a taunt: freedom devalues her; she would prefer to be needed, desired. Certainly her grandson Desmond, who does not rush to visit her, does not need her. As Mrs. Arbuthnot, a Claremont resident, pithily says, " 'The young are very heartless' " (20). And another resident, Mrs. Post, says with unconscious irony, " 'Relations make all the difference' " (10), the irony being that essentially relatives make no difference in these old people's lives—or worse, create additional pain—having abandoned them to an embittering solitude. So Mrs. Palfrey waits in vain through most of the novel for her grandson's visit. However, she does not wait idly, nor does the reader, who learns through Laura Palfrey what it feels like to be alone and old, physically, mentally, and emotionally.

Mrs. Palfrey's freedom in old age thus carries with it the penalties of loneliness and vulnerability:

> Although she felt too old to do so, she knew that she must soldier on, as Arthur [her husband] might have put it, with this new life of her own. She would never again have anyone to turn to for help, to take her arm crossing a road, to comfort her; to listen to any news of hers, good or bad. She was helplessly exposed—to the idiosyncrasies of other old people [Claremont residents], the winter coming on, her aches and pains and loneliness . . . (189).

Her loneliness is underscored here by the passage's contrasting of her present to her "escorted" past. Taylor writes Mrs. Palfrey's bodily response to loneliness at the Claremont, comparing it to the moment she knew widowhood was imminent: "her heart lurched, staggered in appalled despair" (4). Laura even contemplates moving into a nursing home because "anything would be better than being alone" (19). Also eroding Mrs. Palfrey's impulse toward independence is her increasing awareness of her susceptibility to physical ills that hamper mobility. Another resident, Mrs. Post, compares age to the dependency of infancy, " 'As one gets older life becomes all take and no give . . . like being an infant again' " (129–30); the narrator uses the same analogy later: "[Old age] was like being a baby, in reverse. Every day for an infant means some new little thing learned; every day for the old means some little thing lost" (184). Thus Laura sees herself as no longer contributing to society (Leclercq 101), which diminishes her self-esteem. She has in the past lived by rules of conduct: "Be independent; never give way to melancholy; never touch capital" (9). Now in young-old age, she must continually fight melancholy and work to maintain independence. At times she loses independence, as, for example, when she falls twice in the novel and must rely on others to rescue her. Moreover, in her final illness she must use her capital. As the narrator comments, "It was hard work being old" (184).

Yet Mrs. Palfrey does not give up the struggle to shape her life independently even though after her first fall, the effort of walking makes freedom seem like a chimera: "She realized that she never walked now without knowing what she was doing and concentrating upon it; once, walking had been like breathing, something unheeded. The disaster of being old was in not feeling safe to venture anywhere, of seeing freedom put out of reach" (73); under these circumstances, the security of the hearth is tempting. As in many *Reifungsromane*, Taylor writes the old woman's unreliable body here, the fragile bones, the painful varicose veins that curb freedom because "putting one foot in front of the other [brings] pain each time" (24). She describes the strong will that enables Laura to cope with bodily pain while persistently facing the future: "Must keep going, . . . she so often thought. Every day for years she had memorised a few lines of poetry to train her mind against threatening forgetfulness. She now determined to train her limbs against similar uselessness" (108). Here Taylor again writes the aged body, translates words into old flesh by comparing memorization of poetry to exercising of aged legs. To remain useful and optimistic physically and mentally requires Laura's greatest energy and discipline.

Mrs. Palfrey also fights spiritedly against the emotional barrenness of her daily life, against wishing her life away. Filling up empty time is a central challenge for the young old in *Reifungsromane*. But before Taylor shows how Mrs. Palfrey resists boredom, she makes readers feel it by taking them minute by crawling minute through her first evening meal at the Claremont and her next day, up until lunchtime. She details her heroine's activities, showing how she stretches out her unpacking, for example, "so that later might seem sooner" (5). She lists a number of errands planned by Laura to fill the first morning, at the end of which she notes tersely, "She had been out an hour" (9). Mrs. Palfrey's inner monologue is revealing: "She knew that, as she got older, she looked at her watch more often, and that it was always earlier than she had thought it would be. When she was young, it had always been later" (8); and a few weeks later the narrator reports, "Time went by. It could be proved that it did, although so little happened" (23). Mrs. Palfrey fights slow time by carefully chiseling out each day's activities. She enjoys running errands, such as picking up books at the library for the arthritic Mrs. Arbuthnot, and likes to plan routes for her daily walks. She deliberately uses "the little things in life to defend herself against loneliness and despair" (Ringer 2349). What she observes in another Claremont resident, the eccentric Mr. Osmond, who regularly writes letters to the newspaper, Mrs. Palfrey applies to herself: "Action, she thought. He is taking action, he is expressing himself, keeping himself going" (67). Human beings all along the age continuum need to express themselves and to feel that they are productive; Taylor supports and illustrates this idea through Mrs. Palfrey.

Mrs. Palfrey also spends time productively by reminiscing about her years with Arthur. She remembers the early years in Burma where she shared his pride in helping to build the British Empire. These memories of her pride in being English while in a foreign land enable her to reaffirm her identity now: "It had been her solace for homesickness, her defiance from fear, her affirmation of her origins" (104; this affirmation of origins is a major experience for Marshall's Avey Johnson). Mrs. Palfrey also reexamines that part of her identity involved in her wifely role during her husband's retired years in their Rottingdean home, where "the perfect marriage they had created was like a work of art" (64). Through these marital reminiscences, a major element of most *Reifungsromane*, especially those about widows, she accepts her widowhood and revises her self-concept as Arthur's wife; however, this "image of herself" as his widow "seemed diminished: it had lost two-thirds of its erstwhile value" (3). Despite her loss of self-esteem at being a widow, Laura derives joy from remembering the happiness of her past; these memories enrich Mrs. Palfrey's present and rehumanize her, equipping her to fight her bouts of depression, her barren environment, and the hotel manager's insulting treatment of the elderly residents as "naughty children" (199).

Mrs. Palfrey also uses time to enrich herself emotionally by entering into the community of the other old residents; together they form a family, eating meals together and watching the evening "serial." As Florence Leclercq observes, these characters act as foils to Mrs. Palfrey (Leclercq 100); for example, while Mrs. Palfrey is "proud, dignified and reliable like a parade horse" (97), Mr. Osmond is a lecherous old man, Mrs. Arbuthnot is a bitter woman who walks "like an injured insect" and often retreats into her shell of arthritic pain (16), and Mrs. Burton is a flamboyant, extravagantly coiffed, immoderate drinker. Although Taylor only sketches these characters because she keeps readers inside Laura Palfrey's consciousness, each character "is an individual, warped to varying degrees by longevity" (Levin 18). Laura seems less warped by her years, more balanced than the rest. Yet through all of them, Taylor writes variations on the aged body and mind. Settling into this community, Mrs. Palfrey shows a youthful adaptability and the survivor's instinct as when, for example, she cordially meets Mrs. Burton: "She was not the sort of woman, Mrs. Palfrey decided, with whom she would ordinarily have been in company . . . but life was changed, and to save her sanity she must change with it" (15). She has acknowledged that old age makes strange bedfellows. Mrs. Palfrey is part of a class and a world that are vanishing and she realizes she must accept this breakdown of class structure represented at the Claremont (Leclercq 97). In fact, comradeship among the residents transcends English class structure. Although they are not always kind to one another, with their gossip and criticisms, they still recognize each person's individuality, are concerned about each individual's health, and care whether that person is alive, while the rest of the world, including blood relatives, may not. Mrs. Palfrey's Claremont "family" helps to give her feelings of self-worth and belonging, enriches her emotional life.

The most profound way in which Mrs. Palfrey rejuvenates her emotional life in old age is by falling in love with a young man named Ludo. When readers witness middle-aged characters like Jane Somers and young-old characters like Laura Palfrey in the throes of love, they can understand how love, like youth, is often wasted on the young. Through this study of young-old love, the conceptual barriers between youth and age crumble. Moreover, that myth about the Golden Pond mellowness of old age is belied by Laura Palfrey's turbulent, intense feelings for Ludo. Lucy Rosenthal points out that Mrs. Palfrey's relationship to Ludo "has both a filial character, and for her, a dim memory-stirring erotic content" (25). As the erotic content grows, a youthful femininity blossoms in Laura too, challenging common notions of postmenopausal women as asexual or even quasi-masculine; when Taylor first introduces Mrs. Palfrey to us, she alludes to this sexual issue, gently spoofing Mrs. Palfrey's appearance: "She would have made a distinguished-looking man and, sometimes, wearing evening dress, looked like some famous general in drag" (2). Yet Taylor emphasizes Mrs. Palfrey's rekindled girlishness and deepening passion for Ludo after he rescues her from her first fall and becomes a stand-in for grandson Desmond.

The fall-and-rescue scene is couched in affectionate, sexual words that reveal Mrs. Palfrey's dawning love for Ludo: "He took her in his arms and held her to him, like a lover and without a word, and a wonderful acceptance began to spread across her pain, and she put herself in his hands with ungrudging gratitude" (25). As he tends to her wounded leg, the language is again sexual: "She felt no sense of outrage when he lifted her knicker elastic over her suspenders and unfastened her stocking. Most tenderly he swabbed her knee and dabbed it with the . . . towel" (26). Even while in pain, she notices the beauty of his eyelashes and later when she asks him to impersonate her grandson to help her save face before the Claremont residents, she again notices his appearance, this time alarmed by her feelings: "He was almost beautiful, she thought, and the idea so alarmed her that her glance flew away from his face" (33). By the time he dines with her at the hotel, she is comparing her feelings for him to those she had felt as a girl for Arthur (39). Hers is almost an adolescent infatuation—reminiscent of Adams's heroine Laura's passion for Seth and Jane Somers's for Richard Curtis.

Throughout the rest of the novel the young-old Mrs. Palfrey feels great passion for Ludo, intense jealousy of his girlfriend Rosie, and a strong need to forget about him, "like a young girl with an unresponsive, but beloved, boy" (137); Taylor uses several such similes comparing Laura's love to an adolescent's. Ludo is aware that she dotes on him, but he remains attentive to her partly out of a basic kindness that Desmond lacks and partly out of a loneliness not unlike hers. Another reason is that he is a writer and wants to finish his novel about her and life at the Claremont: a *Reifungsroman* within a *Reifungsroman*. His motivation for their friendship aside, Mrs. Palfrey is emotionally nurtured by the relationship. Her feelings for Ludo give her a youth's sense of futurity, sustaining her even on her deathbed so that she no longer believes she is going to die and plans upon her recovery to make him, not Desmond, her heir. All of the stereotypes of the old as desexed and tranquil, as rooted in the past and no longer capable of unsettling passion, dissolve in this portrayal of Laura Palfrey's love for Ludo. With his beautiful eyelashes and gallant courtesy toward her, she simply cannot resist him; readers, having experienced the desperate loneliness of Mrs. Palfrey, readily understand why.

As passion for Ludo and a yearning for companionship beat in the heart of Mrs. Palfrey, Taylor creates the same yearning pulse in Mr. Osmond's heart—for Mrs. Palfrey. Mr. Osmond fights against loneliness and " 'a lack of looking forward' " by asking Mrs. Palfrey to marry him (178). Prompting his inept, unromantic, and almost fierce marriage proposal are: anger at what the years have done, an emotion consistently present in *Reifungsromane* about the young old; youthful resistance against time; and courage in his pipedreaming effort to make a new home and seek pleasure in old age. While he envisions a platonic friendship, believing, like Lessing's Kate Brown, that " 'we are on the other side of passion at our age' " and better for it, readers sense the irony in that statement, knowing of Mrs. Palfrey's schoolgirl passion for Ludo and remembering Mr. Osmond's obsession with telling dirty stories to the Claremont waiters. Although with his lecherousness Mr. Osmond serves as a foil to Mrs. Palfrey's prim dignity (Leclercq 100), he does more than that in the novel: he also reinforces what Mrs. Palfrey's character reveals about young-old people's desire to participate in the full range of human emotions and pleasures and their ability to shape their future—central ideas of *Reifungsromane* about the young old. Leclercq aptly describes the residents' attitudes toward past, present, and future: "The present moment means nothing to Taylor's characters . . . they do not seem to live in the past either, but look forward to some brighter future" (101). While they may be deluding themselves with this optimism, theirs is the "existentialist optimism of those who have nothing to lose" (Leclercq 102). Moreover, the characters' optimism opens them up to a range of feelings that attest to their humanness and enrich it, reminding readers that to dichotomize youth as optimistic and vital and age as pessimistic and inert is invalid.

Thus, when Mrs. Palfrey dies at the end of the novel, readers feel a real sense of loss, like the Claremont residents. This is "not just another old woman" dying; this is a fully realized human being who has lived with courage and dignity, touching others' lives in small ways, coming to understand the design of her own life, and experiencing the wide range of feelings that is the province of human beings, regardless of age. Kingsley Amis has noted that Mrs. Palfrey "is not heroic; she is not called on to face the intolerable, merely the very hard to tolerate" (276), and this is precisely what makes her a believable, sympathetic character. Through her characterizations of Mrs. Palfrey and the other Claremont residents, Taylor enables us to understand what Mr. Osmond means when he observes that "we're all saddled with our hearts" (197): our hearts keep on pumping, as we all keep on feeling and bearing the stamp of our humanity across the age continuum, till we die. Taylor encourages readers to reconceive old age as an opportunity for ripening experiences and intensified feelings. Her *Reifungsroman* fosters the will for social change advocated by Frank Lentricchia: to recast the young old not as unfeeling aliens, but as passional, fully humanized members of society.

BARBARA PYM'S RETIRED WOMEN: INTOXICATING CHOICES AND SPINSTERLY LOVE

Retirement from an active working life is "a serious business . . . that must be studied and prepared for" (100), declares English author Barbara Pym's narrator in *Quartet in Autumn*. But what does this *rite de passage* into young-old age mean for the single woman who lacks the option of retiring to a family hearth? In Pym's 1977 novel, the omniscient narrator lets the reader see intimately, through frequent interior monologues, how two single women, Letty Crowe and Marcia Ivory, deal emotionally and physically with retirement. While in many respects Letty and Marcia are as different as black is from white, as *crow* is from *ivory*, in retirement both women experience an intensifying of their interior lives as they become more introspective, like Jane Somers, Mrs. Palfrey, and other heroines of *Reifungsromane*. Both also attain the sort of optimism regarding their future that people often assume is reserved for the young. Because she is in better physical and mental health than Marcia, Letty Crowe's optimism is less complicated than Marcia's and more observable to readers as the novel unfolds. Marcia's optimism emerges in a more jolting way at the end of the novel.

Letty Crowe's first scene reveals the loneliness of the aging single woman. Letty on her lunch hour at the ironically named restaurant "The Rendezvous" is acutely aware of her isolation from the stranger who sits opposite her; they fail to interact despite their brief eye contact, painstakingly described by the narrator, which Letty thinks indicates their mutual desire to communicate: "Somebody had reached out toward her. They could have spoken and a link might have been forged between two solitary people. . . . Once again Letty had failed to make contact" (4). This shyness has forestalled many potential or incipient relationships in Letty's life. As Jane Nardin has observed, Letty, unlike her coworkers Marcia and Norman, is "willing to take responsibility [that of one human being for another]," but "she has trouble making contact" (131).

Letty cannot even establish close contact with the heroines of the novels she reads and she protests the lack of attention given the aging single woman in literature, positing the need for a new subgenre in modern fiction: the *Reifungsroman*. Pym's tone of amused irony indicates her commitment to this subgenre in *Quartet in Autumn* when her narrator reveals Letty's thoughts: "If she hoped to find . . . [a novel] which reflected her own sort of life she had come to realize that the position of an unmarried, unattached, ageing woman is of no interest whatever to the writer of modern fiction" (3). Pym is determined not only to show that such a woman is of interest to writers like herself, but also to persuade readers that such a woman has intrinsic interest as a human being—despite the fact that "as an aging, unmarried woman of no particular distinction, [Letty] is not wanted by others for friendship and aid" (Nardin 131). In focusing on Letty, the aging single woman, Pym is departing from—and parodying—the English novel's tradition of spotlighting young women in love in *Bildungsromane*. Barbara Brothers has pointed out that Pym's realistic novels chide and satirize novelists for distorting single women's lives and for creating in readers false notions about women living alone: "By not dramatising the life of the unmarried woman or that of the woman who is neither in love nor the object of some man's love, novelists, Pym suggests, have contributed to society's perception that such women have no lives of their own" (63). Pym shows us through Letty that the older single woman lives not a spectator's life but a life of thought, feeling, significant small actions, and growth, a life that engages and touches the reader.

Part of what makes Letty interesting to the reader is her increasing self-analysis, that precursor to change. The narrator first reveals her accepting, positive attitude about her limited life, her tendency not to dredge up the past for examination, but to live unanalytically in her relatively meager present. Letty is a survivor and her accepting attitude has up to now helped her survive. She has adopted an ethic "of stoic endurance and a refusal to impose upon others" (Nardin 127). Yet one of the survival skills she gradually realizes she must acquire is the ability to analyze her past so that she can actively construct a meaningful future in retirement. We have seen this skill developing in Mrs. Palfrey as well as in Lessing's and Adams's heroines, when they reassess their lives with their husbands. Widows and retirees, both experiencing the end of a major chapter in their lives, must take this emotional inventory, and *Reifungsromane* record the stocktaking through internal monologues and flashback narratives.

As Letty starts to reminisce and to analyze why she has had a life so bland and without passion, the reader sympathizes with Letty's bad luck in carving out a fulfilling life, but also becomes a trifle impatient with her passivity, her inability to seize the life that can be hers. As the narrator and Letty compare her history to that of her friend Marjorie, the pattern emerges that despite Marjorie's lack of distinction, Letty, measured against her friend's achievements, always loses. Most obviously, she has remained a spinster while Marjorie married. Letty's self-analysis begins just before her retirement with a dream, common tool to explore the psyche of the *Reifungsroman*'s heroine. In the dream, Letty travels back to her youth and a double date with Marjorie and her fiancé Brian. Letty and her date Stephen do not connect, just as Letty and the woman in the Rendezvous restaurant had not. She wakes up from the dream contemplating what the reader must see as the theme of her life: that people and experiences have slipped through her fingers—in part, she must come to understand, because she has failed to grasp them. At this point of the novel, she just blames her empty history on life's peculiar elusiveness (27).

Letty eventually learns that she has been naïve and romantic in assuming that love is prerequisite for marriage—an assumption supported by those English novelists whom Pym is satirizing here—and that this assumption, together with her passivity, may have contributed to her lonely spinsterhood: "All those years

wasted, looking for love!" (66). Letty's regrets and "half-recrimi-
nations" about not marrying (Graham 155) are deepened by her
dawning sense that she need not have held out for love. Marjorie,
however, learned early to define married love realistically as a stay
against loneliness; she married young and also is about to sidestep
the loneliness of widowhood by marrying David Lydell. Marjorie's
assessment of the basis for her relationship with David is realistic:
they diminish each other's unhappiness. Clearly Pym's contrasting
portrayals of Letty and Marjorie parody "the romantic paradigm
and . . . [Letty's] acceptance of it" (Brothers 79).

Marjorie's new marriage plans compel Letty to reconsider how
she will live since the two women had planned to live together
when Letty retired. The retired, young-old Letty, reversing British
culture's assumption that youth is energetic and age passive, now
becomes more active in shaping her future than she had been in
her youth. First she decides emphatically where she will not live:
she will not, as Marjorie suggests, live in Holmhurst, an old
people's home in the country where she had once seen a disoriented
elderly woman wandering on the grounds (54); Letty is not about
to wander aimlessly in her old age. In fact, she finally shakes off
her acquiescent demeanor and becomes angry at Marjorie for
suggesting that Holmhurst, an environment that would isolate her
more than ever from a vital life, would be good enough for her
while Marjorie would be marrying and starting a new life with
David: she recognizes that although in the past she had followed
Marjorie's lead, she need not "follow the same pattern now" (151).
Letty's introspection has let her see this pattern and Marjorie's
disloyal selfishness, enabling her to reject the pattern and also to
deny age's passivity. Even the language in which she couches her
rejection of Holmhurst is more forceful than usual: "A room in
Holmhurst was the last thing she'd come to—better to lie down in
the wood under the beech leaves and . . . wait quietly for death"
(151). This language is especially strong since life-loving Letty
has not shown any tendency to court death; Letty Crowe will
simply not eat crow any longer.

Even more vehemently she resists continuing the pattern of trailing after Marjorie when her marriage plans fall through. Why should she move to the country and live with Marjorie when she, like Mrs. Palfrey, now questions her formerly professed love of the country? This fondness for the country is associated with the place-by-the-hearth concept of elders voiced by her former co-worker Edwin: " 'But I thought you loved the country,' dismay in his tone, for surely all middle-aged or elderly women loved, or ought to love, the country?" (217). Through Edwin's words, Pym satirizes those comfortable generalizations that reflect widespread yet erroneous stereotypes of retirement and older women. Letty in retirement tries to participate in the life of her London suburb, not wishing to retire from life. She also decides to be herself and to indulge in "selfish" pleasures, reading her novels, buying stylish new clothes, eating good food. Her 80-year-old landlady teaches her by example that self-gratification is an accompanying benefit of senescence, when one need no longer cater to others: "Mrs. Pope did exactly those things that she wanted to do" (142). May Sarton articulates well the self-approval, ripening of capacities, and self-pampering that come with young-old age: " 'I am more myself than I have ever been, . . . more powerful. . . . I am better able to use my powers' " (10). Letty is clearly learning to value herself, fulfill her own desires, realistically assess and tap her powers, and "adapt to [her] limitations" (Kapp 240).

Letty finally realizes that she can do exactly what she wants to do—she has choices—a realization that intoxicates her more than the glass of sherry she triumphantly savors at the novel's end: "She took a long draught of the sweet sherry and experienced a most agreeable sensation, almost a feeling of power" (217); realizing that she can make choices that will shape her future, she is experiencing the heady power of personhood. Having acquired personhood, Letty youthfully anticipates future opportunities for growth. Letty's are the final thoughts of the novel, as she muses optimistically yet realistically on a double-date being planned with Marjorie, Edwin, and Norman (the other half of the autumnal quartet). Acknowledging to herself that Edwin and Norman are hardly the stuff of romantic dreams, she nevertheless manages to conclude with the thought that "life still held infinite possibilities for change" (218). Although she knows Edwin and Norman have limited capacities for feeling and expressing affection, Letty's enthusiasm for the future is solidly based on real changes in her own personality and mode of living, and thus "far more convincing than the conventionally cheery attitudes" she had formerly assumed as her duty (Nardin 134). Letty's future will be richer and less lonely than her past because she is now aware of life's realities and receptive to its surprises.

Marcia Ivory seems to be Pym's foil to Letty. Although she and Letty are contemporaries, Letty retains an air of girlishness and *joie de vivre* while Marcia is the stereotypical old spinster. Dour, rigid, ascetic, and devoid of Letty's interest in the pleasures of novels, good food, pretty clothes, and travel, Marcia once remarks to her coworkers that older people do not need to take vacations (38). Moreover, she is more than shy: she is positively hostile to the friendly overtures of other people, including Letty, her coworkers Norman and Edwin, and the do-gooder Janice Brabner, as if they are invading her secret life with intent to disarrange and harm it. No one really knows what is going on in Marcia's mind because she is very uncommunicative—never having mastered the art of small talk and in fact having disdained it—and few want to make the effort to find out because her anger offends them.

Letty does try to reach out to Marcia in the opening pages of the novel when she senses Marcia's fatigue, offering to make her a cup of tea. But then the narrator reveals that she is repelled by Marcia's eyes, like those of a nocturnal primate (10–11); Marcia seems not quite socialized, not quite human. Marcia also uses dehumanizing animal imagery—but a more domesticated animal—to characterize Letty when she unsociably rejects Letty's gentle offer of tea and sympathy; Pym lets the reader hear Marcia's thoughts about Letty: "She's like an old sheep, but she means well even if she seems a bit interfering" (11). These thoughts reveal Marcia's positive judgment of Letty, but the positive feeling does not reach

Letty to make Marcia more appealing to her coworker; instead Marcia conveys the negative feeling that Letty is meddling in her affairs. Because readers hear her thoughts, however, they understand that there is a relenting side to Marcia's severity. Pym wants to give us a complex character, not just a stereotypical misanthropic old lady, and this is the first hint of the softer Marcia.

There is, nevertheless, on the surface much that is hard, defensive, unemotional, and unfeminine about Marcia. Her unfeminine hardness is reflected in her physical condition: Pym, with intentional irony, writes the old spinster's body, connecting her maimed femaleness to her recent mastectomy, her "breastlessness . . . her imperfection, her incompleteness" (103); everyone in the office knows Marcia is "not a whole woman"; she has lost an essential aspect of her womanhood (9–10). People are repelled by her strange manner, which has become even stranger since her surgery. Readers are initially as offended by Marcia as are the other characters. She seems a mean, reclusive, inactive, desexed old crone, the antagonist of youth. Hence, when the narrator reveals that Marcia, without a relative in the world, had asked herself before her surgery whether her death would matter to anyone, readers might reply, "Not to us" and agree dispassionately with Marcia that if her body were tossed into an incinerator, she would not be missed (20). Yet if we know that Pym began to write *Quartet in Autumn* in 1971, the same year in which she underwent an operation for cancer (Nardin 6), we might expect that she intends a more intense engagement between Marcia and the reader.

Increasingly readers understand Marcia's way of thinking through her interior monologues, and while intimacy does not automatically inspire affection, Pym does begin to make us care about Marcia, as Barbara Brothers notes: Pym's "artistry lies in making us care about those who require the greatest measure of human sympathy—characters neither beautiful nor heroic, neither ugly nor evil" (76). Readers observe with increasing concern that Marcia is physically not recovered from her surgery and her cancer and that she is emotionally withdrawing even further from the world after her retirement, as if the cancer is consuming her feelings too. She virtually stops eating because it takes too much effort to cook, because it would deplete the supply of tins that she stocks and arranges in her cupboard for a rainy day, and because her fantasy life detaches her from reality (including hunger pangs) for long stretches of each day. As readers see her occasionally dining on tea and a tin of pilchards left over from her deceased cat's store only because it does not deplete her own reserves, they recognize how obsessively hoarding she has become, and how without an appetite for life. Her forgetfulness about nutrition and her health suggests that Marcia is self-destructively out of touch with reality; as the narrator reports, she forgets that her doctor has urged her to eat more (87). Scrutinizing the warning on a plastic bag concerning the dangers of suffocation for babies and children, Marcia sounds suicidal as she remarks to herself, "They could have said [keep this bag] from middle-aged and elderly persons too, who might well have an irresistible urge to suffocate themselves" (110). Through the narrator's presentation of Marcia's interior mono-logue, readers learn that this bag is one of many that she has kept scrupulously tucked away from babies and children even though, as the narrator quietly observes, Marcia had not had any children in her house for many years. Her fixation on this bag's warning suggests Marcia's imaginary fears, decreasing contact with reality, and suicidal tendencies. Marcia's suicidal thoughts seem a promise of escape from a savorless existence.

Marcia also withdraws from the world by avoiding contact with her former coworkers. She ignores Letty's note inviting her to lunch and feels threatened by Letty's unhappiness in her bed-sit-ting room because she fears Letty might ask Marcia to share her house with her. Although she does accept the men's invitation to a lunch reunion of the quartet, she bristles with unsociable secre-tiveness when Edwin kindly asks what she has been doing in retirement (134). Her rude defensiveness concerning her use of time reflects both her unsociableness and her inability to account for the large blocks of time she spends dislocated in reverie. And she is not making much contact with her neighbors either, even Priscilla, who, more than the social worker Janice Brabner, worries over Marcia and wishes to help her, but who also understands the need to respect the elderly's desire to remain independent (140). Even she becomes repelled by Marcia's increasingly eccentric behavior. In Britain, a nation traditionally tolerant of eccentricity, Marcia oversteps the limits. Priscilla, for example, is too embarrassed to bring neighbors into her own yard as Marcia digs up her yard in search of her cat's grave.

Marcia's eccentricity and retreat from society are also measured by her total neglect of her appearance, as when the white roots of her harshly dyed brown hair begin to show bizarrely (120). Lessing's Kate Brown made a sociopolitical decision to banish her hair dye with the truth of aging, but Marcia seems too oblivious to reality and the motives for her behavior to make such a statement through her hair. Its condition is just another indicator of how far Marcia has traveled away from the world. When she remembers to change her clothing, she dons startlingly inappropriate combinations of garments; for her luncheon with the quartet she wears a summer coat, sheepskin winter boots, and old mended stockings, and this costume is finished by "an unsuitably jaunty straw hat from which her strangely piebald hair straggled in elflocks" (129). Marcia's clothing shows that she is not only out of touch with fashion, but also with the seasons. Pym's use of the word *elflocks* also suggests that Marcia has become an otherworldly creature. She is the stereotypical dotty old woman, all of her strange propensities intensifying in her retirement.

Marcia's aberrant behavior is clearest in the way she occupies her time in retirement. When the intrusive social worker asks her what she does, Marcia's reply is traditionally female, jarringly inconsonant with her mannish, breastless demeanor and emphasizing Pym's irony in writing the spinster's mind and body: " 'A woman can always find plenty to occupy her time. . . . It isn't like a man retiring. . . . I have my house to see to' " (108). Marcia takes the womanly-retirement-to-the-hearth stereotype to a pathological extreme. Pym satirizes through Marcia her own womanly love of "the orderly and habitual" (Kapp 237) by making Marcia obsessed with putting her house in order. Typically, *Reifungsromane* about

the young old and the frail old depict this physical housekeeping
as a metaphor for the mental and spiritual putting of one's house
in order when death approaches, but the metaphorical significance
of Marcia's domestic activity is problematized by her increasing
dissociation from reality and her unconsciously suicidal behavior.
That her housekeeping reveals her growing mental illness is evident in her collection of milk bottles, which she keeps in a shed,
arranges according to brand, and even dusts occasionally. She
maintains this supply because she fears a scarcity of bottles and
milk during some impending siege or war that she imagines
England would have to endure (64). There are enough bottles in
the shed to last a household two lifetimes, and Marcia does not
even drink much milk, so her siege mentality clearly verges on
insanity. Her extreme annoyance at Letty for giving her milk in an
alien bottle that threatens her careful arrangement and her pains to
dispose of the bottle confirm her madness. Pym implies sardoni-
cally that one may put her house in too good an order to attain real
peace.

On her first day of retirement Marcia gives free rein to another
aspect of her penchant for household arrangement: her sorting of
the drawerful of plastic bags according to shape and size. Readers
see Marcia's mind deteriorating, unraveling, becoming far removed from temporal reality, as they float along the stream of
Marcia's consciousness. The narrator abruptly closes Marcia's
floating reverie with the statement that her first day of retirement
has ended in a flash without her awareness of the passage of time
(116). While Laura Palfrey experiences the crawling of time in her
first day at the Claremont, Marcia's first day of retirement moves
in a cometic streak; Laura's perception of time is common to
Reifungsromane about the young old while Marcia's is an indicator
of her madness.

Marcia's hostile manner and bizarre behavior might prompt
readers to label her as what Simone de Beauvoir in *The Coming of
Age* calls "*another being*," an alien, repellent "old fool in [her]
dotage" (11)—different from you and me. Pym, however, will not
permit this comfortably distant dislike of Marcia; she makes

Marcia not only repugnant, but also vulnerably human by having her fall in love. Like Laura Palfrey, this damaged woman develops a schoolgirl crush on Mr. Strong (variant on Mr. Tall, Dark, and Handsome or Mr. Strong, Silent Type), the surgeon who had performed her mastectomy. Pym's irony in writing the desexed old spinster's body and then plunging Marcia into romantic fantasies effectively dismantles the spinsterly stereotype.

Marcia makes two pilgrimages to Mr. Strong's house, which require quite an effort in her state of health, and simply stands before this "shrine" in reverential awe. She keeps the card noting her next appointment with him in prominent view on her mantlepiece, another object of her devotion; it gives her something to look forward to—May Sarton's criterion for the attitude of the young person. Thoughts of seeing him almost impel her to eat properly. Marcia worships Mr. Strong as if he were God; Barbara Brothers describes Marcia's emotional state well: "Fearful of the world, Marcia has known only her mother and the surgeon to whom she had submitted her body because he was like God, distant and pure" (79). And yet, Marcia's feelings for this "savior" of her body are less reverential and more sensual than Brothers and the pure ivory of her surname indicate. This is no desexed crone; this is a passionate woman engaged in sexual fantasies about a rendez-vous with her lover at the outpatient clinic. She courts him in her fantasies as she seems to be courting death. She has even bought a drawerful of sexy nightgowns in anticipation of her ambulance ride and meeting her doctor in the hospital. She looks forward to entering the hospital, the only place where any man has made Marcia the center of attention.

While Marcia's work had given her no prominence, her "fruit-less and expendable" job having been phased out after her retire-ment (Graham 156), and her private life had not offered any personal satisfaction, no man or woman ever having loved her except her mother, yet in her final illness, ironically Marcia achieves recognition as an individual. As the interns and medical students crowd around her bed to discuss her terminal condition with Mr. Strong, she feels important (173). And Letty thinks enough of her on her deathbed to send her a bottle of lavender water. The fragrance of the lavender water triggers in Marcia's professionally aloof doctor affectionate memories of his grand-mother, drawing him closer to Marcia in her dying hours; he briefly becomes a seven-year-old boy again, and his fond feelings for his grandmother are directed toward the unmaternal Marcia (179). Thus he is there to comfort her just before her death. This spinster has her cherished moments of male companionship.

Marcia's last vision is a lover's vision of Mr. Strong, while her thoughts of her beautiful scar are a tribute to his artistry and his touch on her body. Marcia's final thoughts suggest the strength of her affection for Mr. Strong and her trust, beyond that of her mother, who had feared the surgeon's knife (181). As she smiles affirmingly at him while he stands over her, he exchanges his perpetual frown (and God-like aloofness) for an apparent smile: "he seemed to be smiling back at her" (181). Pym gives her "inveterate curmudgeon" (Kapp 241) this moment of love—or at least a softened Marcia reads affection in Mr. Strong's apparent smile (he *seems* to smile back). The next lines, those of the narrator, indicate that Marcia has just died, emphasizing the importance of this final exchange of smiles with Mr. Strong: it has enabled Marcia to end her life in warmth and dignity, briefly fulfilling her fantasies of love with her handsome surgeon.

Marcia may be mad at the end of her life, but her life in retirement is surprisingly full and contented because of Mr. Strong's presence in it. Although Barbara Brothers argues that Pym "constantly reminds her readers that neither characters, nor love, nor destiny is as grand as it has been portrayed [in fiction]" (72–73), yet there is in this exchange of affectionate smiles between Marcia and her doctor on Marcia's deathbed something grand in its humanness. *Reifungsromane* repeatedly assert that love need not be banished from aging and ailing lives, and Pym has reminded us of its persistent, affirming presence in these lives through her portrait of Marcia. Robert J. Graham's observation about the view of love taken by Pym's spinsters applies to Marcia: "Most recognize such love [by a man] to be an ideal. . . . Most excellent women value even the unreciprocated experience [of love] as part of a full life" (151). Pym's portrayal of Marcia suggests that Marcia valued love and that love is part of a full life, regardless of a person's age and apparently limited social life.

Marcia's love for Mr. Strong humanizes and empowers her in her retirement from work and from life, becoming her major link to humanity, her reason for looking ahead. But Pym's narrator also reveals that she has harbored an affection, though ill-expressed, for coworker Norman. It is first observable during the quartet's luncheon, when Norman urges her to stay a little longer to chat: "A curious expression . . . came over Marcia's face. It could almost have been said that she softened. Had she some feeling for Norman, then?" (135). She reveals that she does only after her death by leaving her house to Norman, relinquishing from the grave "her frantic need to cling to her own autonomy" (Nardin 130). Through this act she finally expresses herself directly, wielding economic power in her bequest and also showing both her coworkers and readers this softer, more generous nature beneath her hard, hoarding surface. She, moreover, empowers Norman, so that he like Letty feels pride, independence, and the intoxication of having decisions to make—whether to sell the house or live in it—choices that will influence his future and the lives of Marcia's neighbors (203). More valuable than the material gift of her house is this resurgent self-pride and power that Marcia's bequest gives her friend Norman. Her gift also connects Norman, as well as Letty and Edwin, to her, more intimately after her death than in life. Norman wanders through the house to which he had never been invited, learning about Marcia's obsessively arranged drawers, her bottles, and her predilection for poetry. And the others help Norman sort through Marcia's possessions, learning how she spent her time and what she thought about: becoming her intimate friends at last.

The irony of Marcia's death bringing these lonely people closer together is evident. Marcia's act has clearly benefited them all, especially herself and Norman, almost as if she had planned it. She had given herself rich fantasies about how Norman might react to the bequest. And she has given Norman, after her death, a means of acquiring new personal dignity as well as a way to articulate some of his feelings for Marcia and to understand some of hers for the quartet. Marcia has helped reclaim for these elders the right to feel passionately, seek pleasures, and have adventures. As they discover a bottle of sherry in sorting out Marcia's things, Norman suggests that they drink it: " 'Don't you think she must have meant it for us, perhaps for this very occasion?' " (216). The reader is now convinced that Norman has the right and the ability to figure out Marcia's intentions; after Marcia's death, their relationship has become more communicative. Moreover, the autumnal quartet turned trio has, as a consequence of Marcia's bequest, become more adventuresome, more playful, more eager to enjoy life's pleasures.

With Marcia's sherry and out of a new sense of power, the trio toast themselves and salute their futures with youth's sense of possibilities and openness to pleasure. In their toast, they abjure life beside a Golden Pond. Letty, especially, has successfully resisted classifying herself as elderly and refuses to equate retirement with stagnation (131, 192). Pym has nurtured in the reader such strong sympathy for these eccentric, active, aging individuals that the customary polarizing of youth and age, represented in the ageistic attitudes and generalizations of the young social worker Janice, becomes utterly repellent to us; Janice thinks "it wouldn't be a bad idea to shove . . . [the elderly] off all together somewhere" (121). Although Mrs. Palfrey's Claremont group shows us how old age sometimes makes strange bedfellows, Pym's quartet doggedly resists the social worker's idea of elders being thrown together to live under one roof just because they are older and retired (121). Like most people, these aging single women and men prefer living alone in privacy and dignity and having the freedom to choose when they will socialize, where they will go, what they will eat, when they will seek medical help—choices that an institutionalized life would prevent. As Jane Nardin has observed, Pym's novel is in part a negative commentary on social agencies' dehumanizing categorization of elders and fragmentation of their lives: "the integrating functions once performed by church and neighbors are now split up among a variety of social service agencies, each of which takes responsibility for only one aspect of an individual's life" (126).

Pym's readers have witnessed too many of the unique thoughts, desires, quirks, and fantasies of these aging characters to accept gross generalizations made by social workers about who the old are, what their needs are, how they differ from the young, and how they should live. Whereas social workers and social agencies might accept a bipolar view of youth and age, perceiving the elderly as case histories that conform to the traits stereotypically associated with old age, Pym's *Reifungsroman* does not. Through interior monologues, especially focusing on Letty and Marcia; through dialogue between various members of the quartet; through the narrator's satirizing of stereotypical images and redefining of meanings associated with spinsterhood, senescence, and retirement; and through Pym's writing of the young-old woman's body, this *Reifungsroman* enables readers to interact with Letty Crowe, Marcia Ivory, and their coworkers as if they were real, complex human beings. We can see aspects of ourselves in them, regardless of our age; as Isa Kapp says, Pym's characterizations enable us to see, across the age continuum, "the risible oddness of our behavior and the miraculous resilience of our nature" (242). Because Pym's novel allows readers to identify closely with these elders, her work thus becomes a force for change in Anglo-American society: readers' perspectives on young-old people have been widened, the barriers between youth and age crumble, and younger people cannot help but engage with individuals in their 60's and 70's, interacting more sensitively with them as neighbors, coworkers, and friends.

AVEY JOHNSON'S JOURNEY TO HER ROOTS: A WIDOW'S SELF-DISCOVERY AND PASSIONATE COMMITMENT TO HER HERITAGE

As the middle-aged widows Jane Somers, Felicia Lord, and Janet Stone Halloran illustrate, widowhood, despite the pain of loss and stress of adjustment to solitude, offers opportunities for reacquaintance with oneself, self-development, and new relationships. The widow reassesses her past in order to reroute her life. These opportunities also offer themselves to young-old widows, but for these older women sometimes the emphasis may be on self-reaffirmation and growth through relationships with a larger community and a larger collective past. These mature women often face and resolve what Erik Erikson has called a "crisis of integrity," characteristic of the final stages of individual development (Skerrett 68), by finding their place in the larger community and by forging a stronger link to their ancestral past. Young-old Laura Palfrey acknowledges her identity as British and in her recollections of her past links herself with the empire-building British class. Paule Marshall's novel about a 64-year-old widow, Avey Johnson, even more dramatically charts her journey toward integration of body and spirit and self-reaffirmation through identification with her community and racial heritage.

The aging Avey, ready, like Letty Crowe and Marcia Ivory, for retirement from her job at the State Motor Vehicle Bureau, is not ready to retire from life's journey. She travels backward and forward along the age continuum as she travels southward in space to embrace her Southern black, Caribbean, and African ancestry with a rekindled ardor. The journey rejuvenates her, restores her health, and empowers her to redefine her mission in life. Eugenia Collier aptly sums up the journey: "The movement of the novel is . . . the achievement of linkages in time and place, linkages of the disparate elements of the individual self as it merges with the collective self" (310). These linkages break down the binary opposition between youth and age, both within Avey and between

Avey and her daughters, turning her into a young-old woman with a mission and a future.

As *Praisesong for the Widow* begins, readers see Avey leave behind her hard-won middle-class security and status, the assimilated world of North White Plains, New York (with emphasis on the *white*) as she disembarks from the cruise ship *Bianca Pride* ("white pride") where she has been vacationing in the Caribbean with two friends. Being aboard this ship represents her having attained upper-middle-class "white" status, once a source of pride to her. Yet she flees the ship halfway through the cruise when it docks in Grenada, fighting against a "peculiar clogged and swollen feeling," a sense of dislocation, of being "not herself" (52); not being herself, or being an artificial, falsified self, has made Avey feel sick. Marshall's narrator suggests Avey's lack of integrity when she says Avey's "mind in a way wasn't even in her body" (10); this mind-body fragmentation—which later in the novel becomes a prominent emblem of what life in America did to the African slaves, the Ibos—here indicates Avey's spiritual enslavement to materialistic white values that have suppressed her "natural" ethnicity over the years. She becomes a *runagate* (the title of the first part of this novel's four-part structure), running away from her white life and moving toward freedom as she begins to purge herself of her artificiality. Dreams of her past, her great-aunt Cuney, and her life on Tatem Island off the South Carolina coast initiate the purgation, and just like Kate Brown's seal dreams, they are the catalyst for additional psychological changes in her. Avey's dreams enable her to recall Aunt Cuney's stories about the Ibos at the Landing in Tatem, stories she had reiterated to inculcate in her niece a racial reverence, a type of African ancestral worship. Recollecting these stories is the start of Avey's reengagement with her ethnic heritage.

Avey's artificially acquired identity is finally dispelled through her participation in the Carriacou Excursion, a trip to a small Caribbean island where people make contact with their ethnic origins, honoring their parents through the Big Drum Ceremony and the Beg Pardon Song, singing and dancing their nations. On

Carriacou, Avey discovers her link to the Arada nation and assumes her true identity by reassuming her true name *Avatara*, for "in African cosmology it is through *nommo*, through the correct naming of a thing, that it comes into existence. By knowing her proper name Avey becomes herself" (Christian, "Ritualistic Process" 82–83). Reaffirmed and energized, Avey at the ripe old age of 64 takes on a new, consuming mission in life: she will be a "myth extender" (McCluskey 333), a passionate witness to her ancestry and a reporter of its riches to her children and the children of strangers. As atonement for her sin of assimilation into white America, she will, like the Ancient Mariner, keep retelling the mythic stories of the yearly excursions to Carriacou and of the Ibos at the Landing in Tatem, thereby helping to keep alive the ties between American blacks and their Caribbean and African kinfolk.

Avey's journey toward integrity and an energizing mission in life begins with her indigestion in the middle of her cruise. Marshall's use of physical illness to suggest the distancing of the widow from major aspects of herself is prevalent in *Reifungsromane* about women before they journey back to themselves. Kate Brown and Felicia Lord become ill and Jane Somers suffers from back trouble; these ills assist them as they journey through the artificial veneer acquired over the years to confront their pasts, become reacquainted with forgotten feelings and dreams, discover new dimensions of their personalities, and affirm their reintegrated identities. Mrs. Palfrey's fall and injury encourage a similar process of self-reacquaintance. The main difference with Marshall's older widow is that in order to achieve integrity, Avey must reestablish ties with her ethnic group. Avey must learn "that harmony cannot be achieved unless there is a reciprocal relationship between the individual and the community" (Christian, "Trajectories" 243).

Marshall also uses an image familiar to readers of *Reifungsromane* to describe the aging woman's self-scrutiny and, often, her self-alienation: a mirror. While at dinner on the ship, Avey stares at her reflection in the mirror, but "for a long confused moment" cannot place herself (48–49). The narrator adds that this feeling has occurred several times recently. Avey staring at her reflection registers the unobtrusive, dignified, assimilated style of the woman, "everything in good taste and appropriate to her age . . . her Marian Anderson poise and reserve. The look of acceptability about her" (48–49); she sees an older black woman whose careful attire and bearing mark her as middle class and acceptable to the white community ("She would never be sent to eat in the kitchen when company came!" 48–49), but at what price? Major aspects of the real Avey Johnson have been buried, and this mirror passage suggests that Avey is losing her tolerance for such self-repression. Avey is preparing to rebel against white society's values and expected code of behavior for the middle-class widowed woman, "the familiar rituals of affluent widowhood—the well-kept home, the well-timed visits from children, the friends retained from habit rather than affection" (Jefferson 403). Her inability to recognize her own reflection in the mirror suggests that she has gone too far in adhering to this repressive code and set of values and is readying herself to break out of the rituals of affluent widowhood imposed on her by white society. She also starts to question the necessity of dressing and acting in ways "appropriate to her age," because she may no longer want to accept American society's censorship of conduct that blurs the distinctions between youth and age.

Her self-alienation and physical illness have surfaced because of Avey's dream about Aunt Cuney, whom she has not thought about for many years. The dream forces her to have the first of three important confrontations with her past: the past of her youth, those memories of her summers with Aunt Cuney on Tatem Island. The second confrontation involves the past of her married life with Jay. The third concerns her even more distant past, that of her ancestors, as she experiences the Carriacou Excursion. As Margo Jefferson comments, Avey "must understand the Middle Passage to take the voyage out: a personal odyssey must acknowledge the historical forces that shaped it" (404).

Avey's dream jogs her memories about Aunt Cuney, a rebellious figure in Avey's family history; she had in her youth been caught doing a forbidden, because non-Christian, African dance step, " 'crossing her feet' in a Ring Shout" during a dance at the Christian Church in Tatem, and had been banned from the circle for one night. "The Spirit moving powerfully in her," her ethnic feelings, had prompted her to dance (33), which was her way of worshipping her African ancestors and of rebelling against the "white" Christian churchgoers in Tatem. Aunt Cuney's impulse to dance as an expression of communal ceremonial worship comes out of the core of African religion, as John S. Mbiti indicates in *Introduction to African Religion*: "Through music, singing and dancing, people are able to participate emotionally and physically in the act of worship. The music and dancing penetrate into the very being of the worshipping individuals" (61). The dance and the legendary quality of the story about Aunt Cuney's conduct reflect the family's cultural ties to the South and to Africa, from which Avey's life in New York is far removed. The "heretical" cast of Aunt Cuney's devotion to her ancestry is made clear by the narrator: "After a time she even stopped attending regular church service. . . . People in Tatem said she had made the Landing her religion" (34). Hers was a religion of ancestor worship.

After the dream, Avey also recollects the reverential story Aunt Cuney frequently told her of the Landing where the Ibos, mystically empowered Africans who "could see in more ways than one," first were brought on slave boats to America. At the Landing, after foreseeing their terrible future as slaves in America, they miraculously turned around and, walking on the water, with Christ-like strength and determination, headed back to Africa (36). Barbara Christian has observed that the story of the Ibos "emphasized their own power to determine their freedom [to return to Africa] though their bodies might be enslaved" ("Ritualistic Process" 76). Their mind/body disunity is evident in this part-slave, part-free condition. It is also evident in Grandmother Avatara's aphorism about herself and the Ibos, constantly quoted by Cuney and the watchword of the novel: " 'Her body she [Cuney's grandmother] always usta say might be in Tatem but her mind, her mind was long gone with the Ibos' " (39). Besides indicating the mind/body disunity, this story reasserts the strength of Avatara's ties to Africa. That Aunt Cuney is committed to enacting and preserving her cultural heritage is evident in her retelling of this folk legend of the Ibos and in her use of black English expressions in retelling it (" 'Didn't want nothing to do with that ol' ship. They feets was gonna take 'em wherever they was going that day. . . . Those Ibos! Just upped and walked on away' " 39).

Moreover, Cuney's intention in telling the child Avey the story of the Ibos is to elicit the same commitment from her niece, to join Avey's mind to the Ibos. As a child, however, her aunt's aim in retelling this story mystified Avey: "in instilling the story of the Ibos in her child's mind, the old woman had entrusted her with a mission she couldn't even name yet had felt duty-bound to fulfill. It had taken her years to rid herself of the notion" (42). Avey never does entirely rid herself of the notion of a mission, for it now resurfaces after her dream. However, it takes Avey the course of the novel to accept her aunt's notion of a mission and commit herself to fulfilling it. Marshall herself is clearly committed to such a mission as a writer. She frequently speaks and writes of American blacks' rich, complex heritage and of her own ancestral debt as a writer to the "kitchen poets," her female relatives who told stories evocative of the past in those kitchens, inspiring her to learn the art of storytelling. The story of the Ibos eventually inspires Avey to escape her own bondage to middle-class white values and reaffirm the values of her ancestors, like Aunt Cuney and her grandmother Avatara, after whom Avey had been named.

In the dream that calls up all of these buried memories of Aunt Cuney, Tatem, the Ibos, and her rich heritage, Avey finally confronts her aunt, who beckons her once again to walk with her through the Tatem fields they shared in Avey's youth. The only problem is that she is clad not in the sturdy high-top shoes and woolen stockings of her youth, but in her chic New York shoes, suit, hat, gloves, and fur stole, reflecting her assimilation into middle-class America. The dream becomes a wrestling match in which Cuney pulls her toward Tatem while Avey struggles against her aunt. Marshall also pulls readers into the dream and evokes its nightmarish quality by describing the physical tussling and fierce facial contortions of the two women and by bizarrely juxtaposing to these events in the dream unchronological elements from Avey's North White Plains past and life with her husband. The effect on readers of the dream's structure is disorienting, typical of *Reifungsromane*, which often redraw categories and blur states of being. Aunt Cuney tears away Avey's refined clothing as her North White Plains neighbors watch her mink stole "like her hard-won life of the past thirty years being trampled into the dirt underfoot" (44–45). By trampling on her mink stole, Cuney is attempting to warn Avey about "the dangers of materialism" (Christian, "Trajectories" 245) and to guide her back to her roots, away "from artificiality, guilt, and self-pity" (McCluskey 333). Aunt Cuney's tearing away of Avey's clothing conveys Avey's feelings of exposure and childlike vulnerability. It is as if by prodding her about her heritage, Aunt Cuney is beginning to strip away the layers of economic security and respectability of her niece's artificial self, which Avey has taken 30 years to acquire.

The second major component of her ritual to purify herself and embrace her heritage involves Avey's confrontation with her husband Jay/Jerome and assessment of her married life. The review of her marriage is a crucial step toward *reifung* for the heroine, widow or wife, of the *Reifungsroman*. Jerome Johnson, hardworking, upwardly mobile, assimilated black man, comes to Avey in another dream to berate her for wasting so much money when she leaves the cruise ship. His return to her in this dream triggers a host of memories in Avey that help her review their shared lives. Even though her husband has been dead over a year, Avey finally is able to mourn her loss of the passionate Jay. Avey also realizes that Jay had died long before the ambitious, cold Jerome. In their early, financially struggling years he is Jay, and their life is filled with music; they routinely dance to music in the privacy of their own room and listen to the praisesongs on the radio every Sunday morning. These music and dance rituals give meaning to their lives by joining them to a collective ethnic heritage: "Something vivid and affirming and charged with feeling had been present in the small rituals that had once shaped their lives . . . to join them to the vast unknown lineage that had made their being possible. And this link . . . had . . . put them in possession of a kind of power" (137). The rituals empower them to affirm their ethnic heritage and give them pride. There is no artificial veneer hiding their ethnic identities during these years.

Avey also reminisces over their joyful, energized sex life, a recurrence of the "remembrances of sex past" motif that appears frequently in *Reifungsromane*. Like the music and the dance, which are actually part of the couple's "love rituals" (Collier 313), the sexual rituals of Avey and Jay nurture Avey at her core and fulfill her identity. Avey recalls how in the heat of passion "she gave the slip to her ordinary everyday self. And for a long pulsing moment she was pure self, being, the embodiment of pleasure" (128). This essential, natural, joyously primitive young Brooklyn self is very different from the cluttered, artificial, strained self of the older middle-class suburban matron. Sensuous pleasures of youth now seem alien to the aging, reserved, puritanical Avey. This reminiscence permits Avey to see how unquestioningly she has endorsed the binary opposition between age and youth and how much she has been inhibited by it.

The artificial "older" self of Avey has developed as the dance, the music, and the passion have subsided, and Jay has become Jerome, committing himself to the hard work and long hours needed to fulfill the American Dream of affluence in North White Plains. Their marriage becomes "a matter of property and propriety" and their "ascent to prosperity [becomes] . . . a concession to bourgeois smugness" (Jefferson 404). Moving through her recollections, Avey is increasingly able to see how high the cost of Jerome's success had been. The italicized phrase *"Too much!"* becomes the refrain frequently punctuating her interior monologue of reminiscence, sometimes plaintively, sometimes angrily, throughout the last chapter of part two (138–45). The phrase carries more and more intensity as Avey remembers and tallies up the treasures of her past that she has lost in their climb to affluence. The reader, now briefed about Avey's rich life with Jay, can see through Avey's eyes that the cost was, indeed, too much. That phrase, repeated three times out of rage at the cost, ends part two. As Jay had become Jerome, so had Avatara become Avey, and now Avey mourns for her earlier married years, angry at the loss both of her husband and of important aspects of herself.

In retrospect, Avey realizes that they could have preserved their youthful openness to joy and pleasure and their heritage, "the most vivid, the most valuable part of themselves" (139), while pursuing the dream of affluence. Avey's frustration and regret ring out in a second phrase, repeated several times and alternating with *"Too much!"*: "They could have done both" (139). But to have done both would have required strength, the awareness of the worth of these passions, rituals, and cultural treasures, and a vigilance over these precious aspects of their lives that Avey did not have at the time. At 64 Avey now knows she must acquire the strength, awareness, devotion, and vigilance. She knows that she must return to the music, dance, and passion.

Avey's retrospective journey to her younger married years has simultaneously moved her forward along the age continuum, leaving her feeling in just a few short hours like "a feeble old woman with a painful lower back and stiff noisy joints" (143). Sixty-four can be old age if one stops looking forward, as May Sarton has told us, and Avey is fixated on the loss of her past at this point of the novel; she feels her future holds only her death. Marshall writes the old woman's body and her perspective in Avey at this juncture, including her wish to avoid seeing her aged reflection in the mirror: "She had no wish to encounter herself in one of the mirrors there. It was bad enough to feel in her bones the old woman she had become hobbling off to her grave" (143). Although she feels old at this moment, in the next segment of her journey she becomes like an infant again; the reminiscences allow her to purge herself of 30 years of her life, in preparation for the new Avey, who will, like a youth, have a future: "her mind . . . had been emptied of the contents of the past thirty years . . . , so that she had awakened with it like a slate that had been wiped clean, a *tabula rasa* upon which a whole new history could be written"

(151). From this point on in the novel, the dichotomies between youth and age are gradually breaking down as Avey is thoroughly purged, mentally and physically, of her North White Plains past, becoming a rejuvenated woman who will write her own future.

Her new history is written in Avey's present during the Carriacou Excursion. The excursion provides her with the third and most intense confrontation, this time with her more distant past, enabling her to greet her future with joy. Through the excursion, Avey returns to the music, the dance, and the passion of her former life. Marshall increasingly uses evocative Caribbean-flavored imagery and lilting Caribbean patois in the characters' names, the dialogue, and Avey's inner monologues in parts three and four, capturing Carriacou's sights, sounds, smells, and natives' rituals. This change in language reflects Avey's intensifying identification with her ancestors and their culture.

Avey accepts the invitation of the aged Lebert Joseph, who like Aunt Cuney reveres his ancestors and is "concerned with identity and its relationship to continuity and regeneration" (Christian, "Ritualistic Process" 79), to accompany him from Granada to Carriacou. Lebert Joseph is Avey's fatherly model of an old person with an uncluttered personality and strong will that give him eternal stamina: "He was one of those old people who give the impression of having undergone a lifetime trial by fire . . . ; using the fire to burn away everything in them that could possibly decay . . . what finally remains are only their cast-iron hearts . . . [steel] muscles and bones . . . the indestructible will: old people who have the essentials to go on forever" (101). He is the sort of individual that would inhabit that new signifying space beyond age classifications, the ageless utopia envisioned by Simone de Beauvoir. He is also able to bridge the distance between the living ethnic community and the family of ancestors. He teaches Avey how to burn away her excrescences so that she too may become a timeless person and possess the same essential character.

The twofold purpose of the Excursion that Lebert persuades Avey to take is similar to Aunt Cuney's purpose in recounting the tale of the Ibos over and over: to allow the younger generation to link once a year to the older generation on Carriacou and also to link the young to their African cultural heritage as they "dance their nation" (164). On Granada, using his patois expressions and rhythms, Lebert introduces Avey to the concepts, rituals, and feelings associated with the Excursion: " 'Is the Old Parents, oui.' . . . 'The Long-time People. Each year this time they does look for us to come and give them their remembrance. . . . If not they'll get vex and cause you nothing but trouble' " (165). Lebert's phrases are sprinkled with black English verb forms and island French as he describes the Excursion, the rituals of placating the Long-time People with roasted corn, lighted candles, and rum sprinkled outside his home, the Big Drum's dance of nations, and the Beg Pardon Song, which he sings for Avey: " *'Pa' done mwe/Si mwe merite/Pini mwe'* " (165). Lebert may have to beg the Old Parents' pardon for misconduct toward them over the past year, but Avey has to beg pardon for her lapses of racial memory over a lifetime. Lebert, with his appealing language, persuades Avey to undertake this pardon and embrace the cultural values and traditions associated with his language.

However, Avey's decision to make the journey is a difficult one; Lebert's invitation immediately summons in her a vision of her North White Plains home and a churning in her stomach that challenges the association of old age with tranquility and reveals her ambivalence about leaving behind her assimilated life in New York. Nevertheless, everything in the novel has been building up to this Excursion—just as all of Marshall's previous novels have thematically led up to this one (Collier 310)—and to the subsequent spiritual "coming home" of the heroine. Avey's stomach unclenches after she decides to make the journey, signaling that her decision is the right one.

The boat ride itself is as difficult as the initial decision to take the trip, but it prepares Avey for the ancestral ritual on the island. The epigraph to this third section of the novel, ending with the boat trip, is a quotation from a poem by Randall Jarrell that suggests what the boat ride accomplishes for Avey; part of the epigraph reads, "Oh, Bars of my . . . body, open, open!" (148). Avey's body and spirit are opened up, making her receptive to the Carriacou ancestral ritual, which will summon forth her pure, timeless ethnic identity. To recreate this dimension of herself, she must become thoroughly unclogged, finish the purging process begun in her reminiscences. The rough seas and crowded deck of the boat purge her forcefully, expelling from her the foul substances, the sick values of her North White Plains years as "Avey." Marshall writes of Avey's physical purification, sparing the reader no detail of Avey's seasickness as she describes the paroxysms, "long loud agonizing gushes" and painful dry heaves; she even analyzes what Avey is expelling: "gouts of churned-up liquefied food" are re-placed by "an endless stream of fluids the color and consistency of a watery lime gelatin . . . mixed with the mucus streaming from her nose and the acids and bile off her raging stomach," which are followed by an urgent diarrhea (204–6). She forces readers to identify closely with Avey in her illness and her exhausting purge. We are as disgusted as she by the foulness of the past that she has expelled from her body/self and as ready to see her filled up with a gloriously pure new substance.

During the boat trip, many of the native women help Avey in her sickness. Avey feels an intense kinship with them and the other Carriacou pilgrims, reminding her of similar feelings of commu-nity when she and her family would journey with other New York blacks up the Hudson River to Bear Mountain in summer: "She would feel what seemed to be hundreds of slender threads stream-ing out from her navel and from the place where her heart was to enter those around her" (190). This childhood recollection of comradeship—another linkage of time and place—further pre-pares Avey for the unifying experience awaiting her on Carriacou.

The unifying threads multiply across generations and cultures when Avey is like an infant bathed and cleansed by Lebert's daughter Rosalie. She removes the last traces of the bodily fluids (and the past) that Avey had expelled on the boat. The lilting Caribbean rhythms and syntax of Rosalie's conversation as she begins to bathe Avey prepare Avey to share in Rosalie's culture:

" 'Come, oui, . . . is time now to have your skin bathe. And this time I gon' give you a proper wash-down' " (217). Avey has cleanly left behind—virtually jettisoned—the unhealthy fat life of North White Plains and is ready, like a baby, to receive the imprint of the Big Drum Ceremony. As Barbara Christian notes, Avey has undergone a ritual similar to "the Haitian voodoo ceremony in which one is washed clean" (154), the *Lave Tete*, which gives part three of the novel its title. This cleansing ritual has completed the purgation and opened the bars of her body, making her receptive to union with others.

Avey and her island kinfolk become one as she witnesses, then joins, the Big Drum Ceremony. During the ceremony, the inverted syntax of the Caribbean islanders and the lively patois increase, suggesting the Caribbean culture's presence alongside of Avey's New York black culture. For example, Lebert says, " '*when you see me down on my knees at the Big Drum is not just for me one. . . . Oh, no! Is for tout moun*' " (236). And patois words form Avey's thoughts as she sees Rosalie at the ceremony: "*Tel pere tel fille. She was unmistakably the old man's daughter*" (216). Another time, as Avey listens to the Beg Pardon Song, she hallucinates, seeing her great-aunt standing beside her (237); again the patois and inverted Caribbean syntax express her thoughts: "it almost seemed to be her great aunt. . . . *Pa' done mwe*. What next was to come?" (237). Aunt Cuney is there because Avey must beg her pardon for forgetting her roots: Aunt Cuney had been the mentor who showed her how to preserve their heritage. The Caribbean patois phrase for "pardon me" is ritualistically chanted by Avey and others throughout part four, reflecting the Beg Pardon Ceremony's central theme of rapprochement between an individual and her ancestors.

Avey watches the old people proudly perform their nation dances, the "bare bones" of their African ancestry (240), and admires the tenacity with which they cling to their ancestry. The rhythms of the spirited Caribbean creole dances, performed by the younger people, also energize Avey. These dances performed by young and old together undermine the binary opposition between youth and age that had inhibited Avey. But the music accompanying the dances also contains a "dark, plangent note," as if Marshall is orchestrating the music to warn Avey, the other participants, and readers about the painful effect of each person's separation from kinfolk or loss of heritage on the "bruised still-bleeding innermost chamber of the collective heart" (244–45). By watching these dances and listening to this music, Avey relearns the history of her people. Avey now recognizes her own need for "the African wisdom still alive in the rituals of black societies in the West" (Christian, "Trajectories" 245). Keeping the African wisdom alive in the people assures an eternal linkage of the generations.

Finally, Avey's heritage speaks to her from the depths of her being, released by the rhythms of the music and the vibrations of the dancers' footsteps: she joins "the endless procession of dancers over the years," spontaneously performing the "Carriacou Tramp" in a timeless trance as she relives in a rush her youthful summers with Aunt Cuney and the Ring Shout dance. Marshall also coaxes the reader to connect Avey's initial dance steps to the Ibos' walk across the water with this analogy: "She moved cautiously at first, each foot edging forward as if the ground under her was really water—muddy river water—and she was testing it to see if it would hold her weight" (248). Her body and her racial instincts compel her to dance her ancestry, in bodily imitation of the psychic process of remembering. As she does the Carriacou Tramp, she carefully follows the rule of not letting her feet lose contact with the ground, a metaphor for not losing contact with her ancestral soil, her people and their customs. Her spirit is with the Ibos now, as reflected in the change in her mouth, which proclaims her ethnicity, "her bottom lip had unfolded to bare the menacing sliver of pink" (247). Now Avey understands the myth of Ibo Landing as "a narrative of resistance, of return as profound resistance and not simply flight" (McCluskey 333). The Ibos resisted their fate as she will resist assimilation into the mainstream culture of America. When asked her name by a stranger at the ceremony, she remembers that she is "Avey, short for Avatara" (251); this rechristening reaffirms her ties to her ancestors, Aunt Cuney, and Aunt Cuney's grandmother Avatara.

As John McCluskey, Jr., has observed, Avey's dancing "defines Avey as a member of a vast family and clarifies . . . her present identity" (333). This dance also rejuvenates her. The narrator describes her youthfulness and strong connectedness to the others: "Now, suddenly, as if she were that girl again, with her entire life yet to live, she felt the threads streaming out from the old people around her. . . . and their brightness as they entered her spoke of possibilities and becoming" (249). Those threads streaming out from the old people to her represent their unifying love across generations and into the future. No longer the old, stiff 64-year-old woman with the Marian Anderson reserve, or the mellow, settled, reminiscing old woman of the Golden Pond myth, Avey has become impassioned, energized, and forward-thinking. All of her—the now integrated Avatara—moves "with a vigor and passion she hadn't felt in years" (249). The freedom and opportunities of widowhood and age, operating within the framework of a nurturing ethnicity, have enabled Avatara to come to fruition. May Sarton offers a personal description of how the acquisition of integrity can give elders a new youthfulness: "Now I wear the inside person outside and am more comfortable with my self. In some ways I am younger because I can admit vulnerability and more innocent because I do not have to pretend" (*At Seventy* 61). Similarly, Avey has made her inside and her outside congruent and has opened herself up to her people with a passion that makes her vulnerable and young. As a result, she is, like Sarton, more innocent and honest, no longer needing the facade that links her to staid, aging, middle-class (white) America.

Avey is also youthfully reoriented toward the future when she channels her ethnic passions into a commitment to her "future role as a myth extender" (McCluskey 333). She will leave behind the white world of North White Plains, retire part of each year to Tatem to reinforce her ethnic ties, and transmit her rich cultural heritage to future generations, beginning especially with her youngest, most passionate and ethnic daughter, Marion. There is a bittersweet irony in this commitment to pass on to Marion tales of the Carriacou Excursion, Aunt Cuney, and the Ibos at the Landing, because Marion had been the unwanted child whom Avey had tried unsuccessfully "to root from her body," just as she had tried to root out her heritage (255). Now that Avey is a whole woman, integrated in body and soul because the values upon which she bases her life are true (Christian, "Ritualistic Process" 83), there can be a stronger tie between her and her daughter, and she can join forces with Marion to teach others the lessons of integrity and ethnic pride that she has learned so well in her young-old age.

Avatara Johnson joins Marcia Ivory, Letty Crowe, and Laura Palfrey in convincing skeptical readers that women in their 60's and 70's may experience new depths of passion and demonstrate courage in looking forward, determined to take on the world, and even to change it. Letty is becoming as youthfully passionate in her embrace of life's possibilities as Avatara is in her embrace of her heritage and the possibilities of passing it on to others of her race. Mrs. Palfrey is as devoted, intense and forward-thinking in her attachment to Ludo as is Marcia in her feelings for Mr. Strong. Three of these women look inward and backward, assessing their pasts, their strengths and weaknesses as people. Then the three look forward, like young people, with the strength that comes from new self-knowledge, committing themselves to a fuller emotional life in the months or years remaining to them. While Marcia in her mental condition does not have their capacity for reminiscence, self-analysis, and new self-knowledge, she is still humanized, energized, and oriented toward the future by a love that only a rare reader would suspect existed in a "sick, dotty old woman." The intimacy and intensity of Taylor's, Pym's, and Marshall's *Reifungsromane*, with their extended interior monologues, strong love interests, evocative dreams, passages of meandering reminiscence, and vivid writing of the older woman's body, open readers' eyes to the ways diverse people in their 60's and 70's think and feel.

By engaging with these heroines and vicariously experiencing their increasing emotional strength and self-regard, readers are compelled to rethink what being 60 or 70 means for individual women. Inevitably *Reifungsromane* reveal the humanity of the young old, the richness and vigor of their emotional lives, and consequently make less tolerable the marginal social status to which elders are often relegated. As May Sarton reminds us in *At Seventy*, "it is possible to keep the genius of youth into old age, the curiosity, the intense interest in everything from a bird to a book to a dog" (76). Laura Palfrey, Letty Crowe, Marcia Ivory, and Avey Johnson all have in them some of this genius of youth. These courageous young-old women philosophically reject cozy hearths, taking to the open road of their futures and pioneering the way to an ageless utopia for all. The *Reifungsroman* is the new generic framework for their odysseys.

4

Challenging Dependency and Embracing Death

Many elders face a time in their lives, whether through illness or the debilitating effects of aging, or both, when they must surrender themselves to their children, or sometimes worse, depend "on the kindness of strangers" to fulfill their most basic daily needs. For some the deterioration suffered is largely physical, and if they have keen minds, their deterioration and dependency evoke anxiety about the loss of dignity and identity. If the physical decay is accompanied by intermittent mental confusion, the dependency, anxiety, and loss of identity may increase considerably. Add to this condition a dread of impending death and we have a grim portrait of old age.

But this is not entirely how contemporary fiction is portraying the dependent elderly. *Reifungsromane* on the "frail old" still depict the mood of adventure, opportunity for growth, and context for intense feeling that fiction on the middle-aged and young old offer. Celeste Loughman's assertion in her 1977 essay, "Novels of Senescence: A New Naturalism," that "there is little in the novels [of senescence] to relieve the dark, unlovely picture of old age" as an "inevitable process of degeneration and decay" (79) is challenged by some angry heroines who struggle with their dependency, demand dignified treatment, crave beauty and love, and contemplate death as a natural ripening process. Two such heroines are Caro Spencer, of American writer May Sarton's *As We Are Now* (1973), and Hagar Shipley, of Canadian author Margaret

Laurence's *The Stone Angel* (1964). With their youthful passion and rebelliousness, Caro and Hagar dispel the polarity between youth and age and insert optimism into the concept of senescence.

Although Caro is 76 while Hagar is 90, both women must accept their physical reliance on others and feel humiliation at this dependency. Yet both adjust without surrendering their integrity, not simply equating dependency with mental and emotional deterioration. In her journal *Recovering*, Sarton recalls how painful depending on young friends was for her as she was recovering from a mastectomy, and she chides herself: "I should have remembered . . . that accepting dependence with grace was one of the last lessons we all have to learn" (Wheelock 426). In fact, Sarton contends that a wonderful intimacy can develop between spouses or friends because of this dependency in old age (Woodward 111). Readers of Sarton's and Laurence's novels can learn how to accept this dependency, returning "to . . . the stultifying helplessness of our childhood" (Springer 48) without relinquishing a healthy self-regard. Moreover, the two heroines' thoughts and feelings reveal: the elements that shape healthy people's identities, regardless of age; the things individuals need to live in dignity; the role love and anger play in dependent elders' lives; and how elders can place death wisely in the scheme of their lives.

In both novels, the journey motif prevails; readers journey backward in time with the protagonists as they try to understand key relationships—especially with the important men in their lives—and unresolved issues and experiences of their pasts. Mary Sohngen has discerned these two related thematic elements in contemporary novels that deal with old age, which are also evident in *Reifungsromane* about middle-aged and young-old women: the life review as a preparation for death and the metaphoric journey toward an understanding of the pattern of life (Sohngen 71–72). Hagar also makes one literal journey while Caro remains basically housebound. In addition to their self-revelations through flash-backs, Caro and Hagar also narrate their present stories in the first person. Sarton and Laurence both use interior monologue to describe the physical challenges of the heroines' daily lives; the emotional isolation; the struggle against losing their memories, reasoning capacity, and contact with reality; their intensifying passions; and their increasing self-analysis. Both heroines reject the polarized conceptions of passionate, active youth versus impassive, inert age. These books do not depict old age as a mellowing period, but as a turbulent one, filled with pathos. They depict two old women who, in the words of an earlier Sarton heroine, Hilary Stevens, retain almost to the end a capacity to care that is "still that of a young girl" (*Mrs. Stevens* 55).

CARO SPENCER'S STRUGGLE TO KNOW REALITY AND ACHIEVE WHOLENESS IN A "PLACE OF PUNISHMENT"

May Sarton is just beginning to receive the critical and scholarly attention that she patently deserves. She conjectures that she has been ignored because she has not been groundbreakingly innovative in her style, nor has her style been in step with literary fashions. Another factor militating against critical notice is that she has never been part of one identifiable group, literary, academic, sexual, or even regional, since she is Belgian-born ("I did not have the advantage of being 'placed' in a regional sense"; Shelley 35). Yet not being part of a group does not bother her because she says she wishes "to be known as a universal, human writer" (Shelley 34). Her universality and humanity are evident in what she calls her " 'J'accuse' " novel about society's treatment of elders, *As We Are Now* (Springer 48). Sarton noted in a 1979 interview that she receives many letters from the young in response to *As We Are Now*. Her portrait of the "embattled old" and Caroline (Caro) Spencer's "guerrilla warfare" militancy (Woodward 110) speaks to rebellious youth. Undergraduate students enrolled in the "Women in Literature" course I have taught generally corroborate Sarton's observation about youthful readers' responses to *As We Are Now*: mine are moved to tears and outrage by Caro's victimization and to applause for her violent retaliation against an ageistic institution; invariably students list it among the two works on the syllabus most likely to influence them in a lasting way. Such responses are not only a tribute to Sarton's universal, human appeal, but also to her capacity for initiating social change by bridging the gap between generations: she is changing youth's attitude toward old age by enabling the young to understand the thoughts, feelings, and goals of the dependent but passionate elderly.

As Letty Crowe complains that the life of an aging spinster is of no interest to the writer of modern fiction, so Caro writes in her journal, which is the framework of Sarton's first-person narrative, that "old age is not interesting until one gets there, a foreign country with an unknown language to the young, and even to the middle-aged" (17). Caro suggests that old age is a subject about which American society maintains an uneasy silence. In her collection of essays about old age, written with Cynthia Rich, Barbara Macdonald also describes this silence: "Nothing told me that old women existed, or that it was possible to be glad to be an old woman . . . the silence held powerful and repressive messages. . . . I had to chart my own course . . . into growing old" (5). And as Pym creates an absorbing tale of two young-old spinsters to counter Letty's complaint of silence, so Sarton writes to show that old age's foreign land is interesting and accessible to the nonelder. Caro's journal is an arresting account of her turbulent life when, after suffering an incapacitating heart attack, she is brought by her also-aging brother to Twin Elms nursing home. Caro's journal is a vehicle that transports us to the foreign country of dependent senescence and translates its language into terms that adult readers, regardless of age, can comprehend.

Caro is in some ways an invalided version of Avey Johnson. As Avey, after extensive reminiscing, journeys toward greater understanding and integration of body and soul, so Caro keeps her journal to travel through reminiscences of her past and analysis of her present toward ordered wholeness and broader understanding: "I am a long way still from . . . the total self-understanding that I long for. . . . I want to get right down to the core, make a final perfect equation before I am through, balance it all up into a tidy *whole*" (18). Caro performs a creative synthesizing act that Kathleen Woodward describes as "the composing of the self" (111). But more than Avey, because she is older and has become frail, Caro is influenced by the prospect of death, which insistently enters into her search for wholeness. Caro intends actively to make herself whole, to change herself inwardly in order to prepare for death: "I have the belief that we make our deaths, that we ripen toward death, and only when the fruit is ripe may it drop" (13). The imminence of death in old age incites a woman to attain true maturity (Woodward 111), brings full *reifung*. Caro conceptualizes death not as the perpetrator of an act upon an unwilling victim, but as a natural consequence of full living, a positive experience sought and created by an active agent.

From the opening pages of her journal Caro demonstrates this active searching, shaping, and ordering impulse—an impulse usually associated with younger women, like the journal-writer Janet Halloran of Alice Adams's "Lost Luggage." That is, the American culture's dichotomizing of youth and age usually makes us associate youth with organizational skill, creativity, and generativity and age with passivity and deterioration. Yet despite Caro's active character, strong creativity, and initial commitment to the search for wholeness, the novel charts her gradual abandonment of her search. Furthermore, she allows herself to be tortured into submission and pushed to the edge of insanity.

The causes of this degeneration of Caro's mind and spirit stem from her institutionalization in "a concentration camp for the old, a place where people dump their . . . relatives . . . as though it were an ash can" (3). Writing in this politically charged language from the beginning of her journal, Caro prepares readers to learn about a social institution's repression of the old, to read a treatise on ageism that "demand[s] analysis of the distribution of social power" (Woodward 108).

Readers expecting to be spellbound by Caro's tale of her cruel victimization by the power structure at Twin Elms may, however, be arrested by her journal's opening line; this line seems either to manipulate readers into a feeling of sympathy for the beleaguered

Caro or, unintentionally on Caro's part, to cast doubt on her reliability as a reporter of reality. She begins with, "I am not mad, only old" (3). An initial reaction might be, how sad that she must defend her sanity in a society that, as de Beauvoir has suggested, often equates senescence with dotage (de Beauvoir 11). Yet readers may wonder whether her denial of madness is meant to alert them to symptoms of incipient mental breakdown, her increasing inability to distinguish between what is real and what is hallucinated. Caro feeds readers' suspicions a few paragraphs later by stating, "Sometimes old people imagine that everyone is against them. They have delusions of persecution. I must not fall into that trap" (5). This statement may disarm us of the suspicion that Caro is subject to paranoia, since she claims to be on guard against it. Yet the suspicion soon resurfaces when she candidly admits that she loses track of time during her mental wanderings (9). Moreover, she displays what might be construed as paranoia when she says of Harriet Hatfield and her daughter Rose, who run Twin Elms: "The two women are always in and out of every room, and one never knows when they are listening" (12). Do readers have to sift through what Caro reports, separating the real from the imagined? What is real and what is hallucinated? Readers increasingly ask these questions.

Sarton may want Caro's text to enable readers to experience an elderly person's lapses into mental confusion and anxiety about the unreliability of her own senses in perceiving reality. Experiencing such sensations through Caro's journal may be a young or middle-aged reader's ticket into the foreign country of senescence. Caro confesses: "The borderline between reality and fantasy is so thin in this confined, dreadfully lonely place" (20). Her repressive environment as well as her age may cause Caro's mind at times to play tricks on her, just as her narrative may deceive the reader, so that both Caro and reader wander in a twilight zone between reality and fantasy, between rationality and senility. In creating this twilight zone, a new space for most readers, Sarton is infusing them with imaginative sympathy for the institutionalized old and breaking down the barriers of fear and antipathy between younger and older.

Given this narrative framework, what can readers learn about the horrors of institutional life for a dependent elder, as Caro conceives them, and what advice can Caro give about fighting against these horrors? The cruel mind-games of Harriet Hatfield, the powerful "warden" of the helpless "inmates" in this "prison," are the worst of the horrors that Caro endures. Caro writes that Harriet is trying to possess her mind and heart, to brainwash her, to break her spirit and make her lapse into passivity. She enjoins herself to resist taking the tranquilizers Harriet gives her when she is feeling weepy or angry and to fight the mental fuzziness and apathy to which Harriet's drugs and threats of solitary confinement reduce her. She writes in self-defense: "All I have is my mind and I must keep it clear. Remember that, Caro. *Don't let them steal your mind*" (23). Harriet expects her elderly charges to feel that Golden Pond mellowness and assumes that they have neither the range nor the intensity of adult emotions (55). Caro denies the Golden Pond myth, claiming that she is as capable of feeling as she was at 21, despite her physical age; in fact, she continues, "I feel things *more* intensely than I used to, not less. . . . But how many old people *are* serene?" (75). Because Caro feels intensely, she violates Harriet's precept that wellness for elders at Twin Elms means passivity; hence Caro is assumed to be crazy and dangerous and must be contained or broken (72).

To punish Caro for her intensity of feeling, Harriet plays one especially cruel mind-game. She tries to make Caro feel mad, incompetent to judge what her "failing" senses tell her is real, by lying to her—or at least Caro insists in her journal that she is being lied to: "I think they want to persuade me that I'm not quite sane. . . . Harriet tells me I have done something . . . or said something . . . that I cannot remember *at all* . . . what happens next is a growing distrust of everyone and everything" (39). That growing distrust of all extends to her own failing mental faculties. Harriet's lies about Caro's mental incompetence are damaging to Caro's psyche. Through Harriet's deceptions, Caro undergoes what

Woodward describes as her "initiation into evil," whereupon she
gains perception "at the expense of personal and social catastrophe" (121).

Struggling against Harriet's alleged lies about her mental incompetence, Caro has few opportunities to verify reality because of her
social isolation, a prevalent theme of *Reifungsromane* about the
young old too. Few people visit Twin Elms; those who do are
influenced by Harriet's view of Caro: " 'Poor Miss Spencer,' I
heard Harriet say to some visiting relative, 'she means well, but
she is quite cuckoo. We have to warn people against anything her
deluded mind makes her invent against us' " (64). Thus Harriet
undermines Caro's testimony about the cruel treatment of Twin
Elms residents by persuading outsiders to question her powers of
observation. Caro acknowledges as the worst torture Harriet is
inflicting on her "the torture of not being *believed*" (71). Lucidly
she explains that no one will believe her when she describes events
at Twin Elms because "they are building up an image of me [as
crazy] . . . that will brainwash anyone who tries to come close"
(71). Despite her explanation, however, readers may prefer to see
Caro as crazy—to view the horror of Caro's tale as exaggerated:
it would be less threatening to a younger reader if Caro's story were
an exaggeration of the indignities of nursing home life.

If Harriet is telling the truth, then interpreting Caro's claim of
Harriet's harassment becomes problematic: "They gave me salt
instead of sugar for my coffee this morning. On purpose? I rather
think so" (65). Is Harriet deliberately upsetting Caro, is Caro
paranoid, or are Caro's taste buds confusing her? It is a fact that
the efficacy of elders' taste buds diminishes. Or perhaps Harriet
made an honest mistake rather than trying to vex her. On the other
hand, Harriet may, in order to debase and render her residents more
pliable, calculatingly deprive Caro and the others of the physical
"luxuries" that make life bearable for the infirm elderly: pleasant
smells, gentle handling, the kind of care that makes them feel like
dignified human beings. Caro describes the soiled sheets, the
stench of urine, and the rough physical contact; she feels as if she
has been assaulted when Harriet washes her hair (71). Yet Caro

may be imagining or exaggerating such mistreatment. Readers learn how difficult it could become for dependent elders to gauge reality accurately.

Whether or not this rough treatment really exists to the brutal degree Caro describes, it is important that Caro perceives the treatment as brutal and dehumanizing. Her pride suffers and she feels her identity slipping away. An image present in most *Reifungsromane* is used by Sarton to describe the negative effects of institutionalization on Caro's identity and self-respect: a mirror. Caro writes: "my face . . . startles me each morning. Can this worn-out, haunted old body be me? . . . Better turn the mirror to the wall" (23). The mirror helps Caro see the old woman's body, while her journal writes both aging body and faltering mind. The journal asserts her pride of ownership in her body, which she can still wash by herself (12); but further translating word into flesh, it also records, like most *Reifungsromane*, "all the horrors of decay," the wrinkled, liver-spotted skin (74) and her body's unreliability: the falls and bruises (8, 54, 66), the irregular beating of "that testy animal," her heart (54). In addition, in the journal she records her precarious mental state, the turmoil and feelings of panic, by describing her claustrophobic nightmare-dreams of locked airless corridors and using images of whirlwinds, "troubled oceans," and drowning (66–67). She can no longer say with pride, "I'm myself alone" (17) and doubts her ability to achieve integrity: "Far from making myself whole . . . I am sinking into madness or despair, fragmented, disoriented" (67).

Caro tries to fight this despair and fragmentation in five ways: through keeping the journal; through maintaining and refueling her anger at her unjust treatment; through reminiscing about relationships from her past; through reaching out to the other residents, the local clergyman, his daughter, and Anna Close; and, as Macdonald observes, through planning, without fear, her own death (99).

According to Kathleen Gregory Klein, Caro writes her journal "to distill experience" (152), like Janet Halloran in "Lost Luggage." She also writes for a political purpose: to expose publicly Twin Elms's atrocities against the elderly after her death and to denounce "our cultural devaluation of the elderly" (Woodward 115). But her writing, in addition, eases her anxiety about her deteriorating mental faculties. She explains how her journal provides a check against the distortions of solipsism, allows her to verify her rational existence—a Cartesian "I write, therefore I am": "It is far more substantive than . . . my most intense thoughts . . . because I can see it and read it *outside* my mind, I know that I exist and am still sane" (40). Caro likens the old woman's mind to "a body out of training," for which daily journal writing will tone its muscle (30); Mrs. Palfrey uses the same analogy, reversing it, so that she trains her limbs as she had daily trained her mind by memorizing some poetry (108). In many *Reifungsromane*, the "body remembers *for* the mind," as Caro says (55), or the body and the mind analogically write (compose) each other.

When Caro claims that the journal testifies to her sanity, however, she does not consider that once a text is created, readers may interpret it according to their own psychological and cultural framework. Caro may need to see sanity in her entries, but as mentioned earlier, a reader may find evidence that casts doubt on the reliability of Caro's rational faculties. As Robert Scholes notes in *Textual Power*, when we are interpreting a text, we are laboring to create meaning, to make "connections between a particular verbal text and a larger cultural text" containing our culture's values and beliefs (33). If our culture maintains that senescence and dependency are equivalent to senility, we are more likely to read senility in Caro's scribblings. Furthermore, a reader may proceed beyond interpretation to Scholes's deeper level of criticism, asserting his or her own power against the power of the text, making "value judgments" that may lead to "a critique of culture" (Scholes 35, 38, 43). Then that reader might resist Caro's aim of persuading her audience to denounce American society's institutionalization of the old, but might, on the other hand, question society's criteria for distinguishing lucidity from senility, for determining the distinctions between internal and external reality. Thus one could see in Caro's text the brilliant insightfulness of a mind even as it wavers between rational lucidity and hallucination. No matter how a reader interprets and criticizes Caro's text as a measure of her accuracy in grasping reality, however, the therapeutic power of journal keeping for Caro is still undeniable, particularly in its capacity to sharpen her memory (Macdonald 95) and help her resist victimization.

The second way in which Caro fights disorientation and fragmentation is through an energizing anger. When she rages about her dependent condition and cruel manipulation by Harriet, Caro at first feels ashamed of her anger, out of control, and unlovable: "All my life anger has been my undoing . . . I must begin the serious work of self-making that will conquer it forever" (36). Yet in her moments of perceptivity and self-acceptance, she attempts to nurture rather than conquer this anger, using it to help her "take charge of her life and her own dying" (Macdonald 94) and reassessing it as justifiable, or even righteous indignation. Her language is religious as she sermonizes herself: "Caro, try to think now and then that you are a human being full of unregenerate anger and sometimes inhabited by sacred fire" (38). This sacred fire is the rage in Caro that longs for divine vengeance against Twin Elms. Rather than stoically enduring her humiliation there, Caro is impelled by her wrath to resist, to engineer "a cleansing holocaust" (106). Woodward sees Caro's burning of the home as "a fiery protest against inhumane conditions . . . an act of responsibility" (121–22). It is also an act of individual courage that invests Caro's life with meaning; as Macdonald says, "Caro is not afraid to die, so in a way never possible before she is not afraid to live" (99).

Again, a reader may wonder whether Caro is choosing violence as an act of social conscience, a political solution to the burden of oppression (Woodward 122), or whether the rage has driven Caro mad. Perhaps she is the only sane one in her world, like a biblical prophetess who, seeing the corruption at Twin Elms, prays for lightning—an act of God—to burn down the place, but meanwhile gathers lighter fluid, candles, and matches in case she herself must do the scourging. A reader may be convinced of Caro's madness in plotting violence when near the end of her journal she acknowledges the loss of identity that betokens her mental breakdown: "That person [Caro] has ceased to exist. Someone else, mentally ill, tortured, hopeless, has taken over my body and my mind" (103). Yet earlier, when more in touch with her mind and emotions, she rationally articulates her political commitment to violence to change her intolerable situation, observing that "things can be changed here, but only by violent action . . . if I burn the place down some day, I can open this locked world—at least to death by fire, better than death by bad smells and bedpans and lost minds in sordidly failing bodies" (83). If one cannot ripen toward death in a fruitful way, reasons Caro finally, then death with dignity by suicide is preferable to death in abject humiliation. She will rage against the dying of the light and go out in a heroic blaze (114–15). Such reasoning sounds sane, if radical in its absolute idealism. The truth may be that Caro blurs the distinctions between political rationality and impassioned madness in her crusade against Twin Elms. Sustaining her anger is, nevertheless, a way of maintaining integrity and fighting against despair.

Anger is a good antidote to despair and fragmentation. Thus it is central to *Reifungsromane* about dependent elders, perhaps as a reaction against patriarchal society's fear of old women and impulse to deny, curb, or trivialize their anger (Rich 84–85). As Cynthia Rich says, for an old woman to express anger at mistreatment and unmet needs is an act of great courage, "so dangerous is her world, and her status in that world so marginal" (85). *Reifungsromane* conceptualize fictional old women as angry, liberate them from strictures about expressing it, and provide a forum for the anger so that other women can read about it.

Recollections about key people in her past, like Aunt Isabel, also help Caro to build her self-respect and integrity. Reminiscing about Aunt Isabel, furthermore, justifies her rage and plan to destroy Twin Elms. Aunt Isabel is a role model for Caro just as Aunt Cuney is for Avey. Caro thinks and writes about this outrageous eccentric of her family, who remained single, earned a Ph.D. in political science, achieved fame and success, flouted conventions for women, and lived with gusto. Thoughts of Aunt Isabel diminish

Caro's self-recriminations about never marrying. Caro confesses to having been enamored of Isabel's style and way of life. She fantasizes about how Isabel would react to Twin Elms: "Oh, what I wouldn't give to have her sail in here and demolish the place by the sheer force of her personality! She would have carried me off without a moment's hesitation!" (81). Because there is no strong heroine, no Isabel to rescue her from degradation, Caro visualizes herself in the heroic role, inspired by this reminiscence. Caro is convinced that Isabel would support her criminal resolve to cleanse Twin Elms of its corruption: "I can hear her saying, 'Only cows go meekly to the slaughter. You're a brave woman, Caro. And you're not crazy enough to let them . . . carry you out addled and totally gone to seed . . . you'll go out in a blaze!' " (118).

Such heroic conduct is the stuff of fiction, but is setting her world on fire normal conduct for a real woman in a nursing home? Caro's reminiscence about her aunt energizes her, but she may be deluding herself by imagining Aunt Isabel's approval of her violent plan. Her reminiscence raises additional questions about her mental stability and about Sarton's intentions behind the fictional mask of Caro as journal writer. Readers may wonder whether they are supposed to view Caro's fictional world as realistic. If so, then the next question is whether to sympathize with Caro's despair so thoroughly as to condone her plan to destroy Twin Elms and all its inhabitants; to condone it, one would have to see it as Woodward does: an act of "collective euthanasia" (122). Others might see her plan as premeditated murder, rejecting as presumptuous or mad Caro's claim that "the old men are better off dead" (118). Readers' sympathy for her despair may also be tempered by the suspicion that Caro has fantasized or exaggerated the conditions summoning the despair.

As recollections of Aunt Isabel prevent Caro from sinking into apathy, so memories of her British lover Alex prevent Caro from sinking into self-loathing. As Marlene Springer has observed, many of Sarton's elderly heroines preserve their dignity and revive their sense of themselves "through what Sarton calls 'floating,' allowing the mind momentarily to range freely over the past and in so doing integrating the present" (48). "Floating" is a salient characteristic of *Reifungsromane*, experienced also by Mrs. Palfrey, Kate Brown, Marcia and Avey, among others. Caro's mind floats over her first meeting with Alex, their shared picnics and conversations, their letters to each other and his fostering of her self-worth: "I felt cherished and admired" (25). As she rethinks the moot question of whether she ever wanted to become Alex's wife (he is married and does not want to divorce his wife), she confronts the fact that she would not have liked or met her wifely responsibilities gracefully (26). Caro understands, finally, that it was right for her to remain single; she chose not to risk giving up her authentic character by marrying (89). Sarton suggests that this opportunity for reminiscing is rewarding: old age "gives us the leisure and the freedom to venture into such fragile, unexplained areas of our history, to return to missed possibilities, and . . . to order the present" (Springer 48). Recollections about Alex—remembrances of love past, a familiar feature of *Reifungsromane*—have helped her to put part of her life in perspective. Caro has also been reminded that she was and could still be a lovable, whole person. She completes this "journey into the heart land" (27) with a sense of peace that helps her through the moments of helpless rage, self-doubt, and self-hatred at Twin Elms.

Four people in Caro's present life also help her to maintain some affection for herself and a steadier grasp of reality: Standish Flint, by refueling her hatred of Twin Elms; and the other three, the Reverend Thornhill, his daughter Lisa, and Anna Close, by eliciting her affection and love. Standish Flint is a stoic resident at Twin Elms who maintains his integrity and dignity despite much physical suffering. Caro admires him and feels a kinship with him: "Like me he cannot be beaten down yet. He is still his own man" (12). She observes that because he, like herself, refuses to maintain the passive demeanor of the other residents, Standish is punished in subtly cruel ways: for example, his requests for the bedpan and other necessities are deferred (12). He resists the staff by refusing food and throwing away tranquilizers and, like Caro, by keeping mentally alert through anger: "What keeps him alive is a deep, buried fire of anger. . . . He is always planning a way to get around 'them' . . . by sheer tenacity, by passive resistance. . . . 'They won't get my head,' . . . 'They won't castrate me . . .,' he whispers" (19–20). Standish's presence is a comfort to Caro. He actively rebels against his oppression, showing Caro how to survive intact at Twin Elms despite humiliation by Harriet. He is also a comfort to her because she can feel useful when she defends him against Harriet: "I have needed the illusion that I could still be . . . needed by someone" (62).

Another survival tactic that Caro tells us Standish uses, like Mr. Osmond in *Mrs. Palfrey at the Claremont*, is escape through sexual fantasy and scatological jokes, some about Harriet and Rose. Caro also has pleasurable, self-affirming sexual fantasies about Alex. The sexuality of the old is still a source of discomfort for many people who accept American culture's polarizing of erotic youth and asexual senescence, and people ease their discomfort by joking about "dirty old men and women." Yet *Reifungsromane*, mirroring reality, consistently demonstrate how central sexuality is to a human being's life even in senescence, both sexual activity and reminiscences about previous sexual relationships ("remembrances of sex past"). Sexuality is an affirmation of one's humanness, a declaration of optimism about the potential and the desire for interaction with others. Sarton's depiction of it in elders is, as Woodward suggests, an implicit "critique of our cultural devaluation of the elderly" (115). While readers might not think of the flinty Standish, stone-deaf, bedridden, in pain, "tart and bitter" (19), as having sexual fantasies, or even as showing a softer, more companionable side, Caro does; recording his portrait in her journal, she undermines stereotypical assumptions concerning this "dirty old man."

Standish's death without dignity and alone in an ambulance on the way to the hospital profoundly upsets Caro. She learns from Standish's death that it is virtually impossible to make oneself whole and die intact, uncastrated, in this institution. His death is a perennial reminder to Caro of all that is wrong with Twin Elms; he is the flint that repeatedly sparks her anger and sustains her plan to set fire to the home.

In contrast, visits by the Reverend Richard Thornhill and his daughter Lisa are treasured by Caro because they ease her anger. They also diminish her sense of helplessness and fear of mental deterioration. When she speaks to Mr. Thornhill about what goes on at Twin Elms, she relishes the fact that she is believed. He quickly acts on her words by contacting the state medical inspectors (who only temporarily make a change in the place). Lisa helps Caro to communicate with the outside world by mailing her letter to Caro's old friend Eva, by bringing her books and flowers, and by honestly conversing with her. The images Caro uses to describe Lisa's visit—for example, the fresh smells of the roses and mums she brings—contrast with Caro's flat images of institutional life: bad smells, her skin "parched like a desert," plastic ware for meals, white mashed potatoes and "colorless meat" (60), all of which reflect her sensory deprivation. She exuberantly writes that Lisa has physically refreshed her (60).

Both Lisa and her father have taken the time to penetrate the mask of old age and have met the lively, intelligent, ageless woman behind the mask. In his last visit to Caro before her death, Richard Thornhill praises Caro's moral strength: " 'I have seen in you what courage can be when there is no hope. I have seen the power of a human being to withstand the very worst and not be corrupted, and not change' " (125). It is as if he is eulogizing her in these words, glossing over the fact that while she has not been corrupted, she has changed—as she readily confesses; she is stripped bare and in a state of despair akin to madness (120). His warm sentiments have, nevertheless, enabled Caro to depend on him even while her world is crumbling around her: she entrusts him after her death with her journal, requesting that he publish it to expose the truth about this Hell for the elderly.

Caro is also temporarily kept from despair, dehumanization, and mental deterioration through her relationship with Anna Close, the woman who substitutes for Harriet when she is away on vacation. Close is how Caro becomes to Anna, a woman with kind, gentle ways who treats the elderly residents with humanity, who gives Twin Elms a cleaning in more ways than one. She nourishes Caro's starved senses by giving her a pink rose and lining her breakfast tray with a pink cloth—she is her divine nurse, affirming Caro's womanly (pink?) worth and allowing her to feel love again (76–77). Caro drinks in the beauty of the rose, lying in bed for an hour really attending to its appearance and scent intensely. Such intense joy in observation is "a reward for the maturity of old age—the ability to concentrate on a single, special item and appreciate it fully" (Klein 151); this is the same "real slow full enjoyment" that Jane Somers learns from the very old (Lessing 166). The rose is also suggestive of romantic love, the feelings Caro develops for Anna, ironically the opposite of her feelings for Harriet's daughter Rose.

Just as intense as her viewing of the rose is Caro's blossoming love for Anna. Although at first she fears having such strong feelings for Anna ("Don't make a fool of yourself, Caro! Old people . . . get infatuated easily"[78]), Caro decides that she has a right to feel intensely because she is human, despite society's ageistic cautionings about elders' feeling anything but serenity or mellowness: "the heart and its capacity for suffering and for joy never dies. . . . The sin would be to stop loving . . . I can still respond to life in a normal human way" (78). Love's persistence challenges the dichotomizing of youth and age: it is a natural, humanizing impulse, regardless of one's age, as Laura Palfrey, Marcia Ivory, and Caro teach readers. Sarton is very clear on this theme of love in old age. In earlier novels such as *Kinds of Love*, she consistently affirms that "love in old age is still vital" (Sibley 140–41). Charles Feldstein, Sarton's adopted brother, wrote words of tribute to his sister on her 70th birthday that are relevant to this theme: "Adventure is proper for this special birthday because of the adventures which lie ahead for you. And also because you taught those who love you that despite chronology, adventure is here for those who remain open to love" (*At Seventy* 15). Sarton herself has remained open to love, as her journal *At Seventy* frankly reveals, and she is determined to show readers of

Caro's journal how passion operates in elders. She suggests that Americans are particularly susceptible to misperceptions about this subject:

> I want to say to Americans, don't think that people are dead when they're sixty because they're not. The more we learn about gerontology, the more it becomes clear that people go on having a capacity for passion, love, really, into their eighties. This shocks Americans to death. . . . They think that . . . when you retire, you retire from everything (Shelley 39).

If as Caro declares, "hate is corrosive" (85), then love is restorative; her feelings for Anna make Caro " 'feel ten years younger' " and eager to live (86). This view of love, shared by Felicia Lord, Jane Somers, and Avey Johnson, is central to many *Reifungsromane*. In describing Anna's kindness to her, "being cared for as though I were worthy of care . . . treasured" (86), her use of the word "treasured" is comparable to the word "cherished" in her reminiscences about Alex, revealing the depth of her love for Anna and its romantic, erotic elements. This love has the power to "make all things new"; she uses quasi-religious language to describe it: "[True love] always comes as revelation, and we approach it always with awe" (93). The regenerative, miraculous power of love is evident in the letter Caro writes to Anna after she has left. Her love for Anna is comparable to her love for Alex, even though the time span of the second relationship is much shorter, because time has become concentrated for Caro—"a time of pure presence" (Woodward 111)—and more intense feelings and experiences are crammed into shorter periods. She also has more time for intense feelings now that life's routine activities are over. Time frequently comes under scrutiny in *Reifungsromane*, but time does not crawl for Caro as it does for Laura Palfrey, Maudie Fowler, and other elders because of Caro's intensity and the extreme conditions of Twin Elms. Caro's gift to Anna of a blouse she had bought years ago to please Alex indicates the fervor of her new attachment: "the blouse . . . comes from my old love to you, my miracle of new love" (99). Love is always treated with this reverence in Sarton's works, as are those characters who feel, give, and receive love. Marlene Springer comments on Sarton's exploding of the Golden Pond myth: "That at seventy all eroticism, possibly all emotion, has not mellowed into what is euphemistically called peace is one of the positive possibilities of aging that Sarton offers" (48).

The return of corrosive hatred, humiliation, guilt, and self-doubt, after this miraculous love, breaks Caro. Harriet reads Caro's letter to Anna and attacks her, dragging this love into what Harriet imagines as a sordid realm of lesbian "dirt" (100). Being bisexual herself and forthright in her endorsement of love between human beings regardless of sex (Bakerman 88–89), Sarton is clearly offering in Harriet's attack further evidence of her smallmindedness, intolerance, and cruelty. Caro must endure the otherness of being old and the otherness of her lesbian feelings, which are conflated: "For Caro . . . the accusations of the 'sickness' of lesbianism and the 'sickness' of age become one" (Macdonald 96). Harriet's attack on Caro's love undermines Caro's identity: " I do not address myself any more as Caro. Caro is dead. . . . Someone else, mentally ill, tortured, hopeless, has taken over my body and my mind" (103). Another Caro embraces hatred and despair in her plan to destroy the nursing home and overcome the evils of this institution: "The institution's systematic repression of the positive, uniting forces of love necessarily generates an equal and opposite force" (Woodward 123). From this point on, Caro is "dying for lack of love" (110), which all need to survive. If she continues to live loveless, she cancels the validity of her life. So Caro now focuses on validating her life, planning "her own emotional salvation," through the fiery destruction of herself and Twin Elms (Klein 152).

Although at the opening of her journal, Caro declares her intention to make herself whole and ripen toward death in a fruitful way, she concludes that the institution of the nursing home blocks this goal. Her decision to end her life before becoming whole is forced upon her when Harriet reads her journal; her very self has been violated, and Caro must respond by reaffirming her integrity and control of her life through suicide (Bakerman 88). Yet, by taking control of her own death, Caro in another sense becomes ripe or fully mature at the end of her life. She disengages herself from human relationships—the ultimate jettisoning, which Elisabeth Kübler-Ross says terminally ill patients perform in the latter stages of dying—and enjoys what she determines are the greatest nonhuman treasures of her life: nature, music, and poetry. She describes her liberating ritual of weaning herself away from her earthly existence and savoring the remaining essence: "I feel free . . . I rejoice as if I were newborn, seeing with wide-open eyes, as only the old can, . . . the marvels of the world. . . . (The human world in the sense of relationship is not mine to worry about or to partake of any longer . . .). I am gathering together all that matters most, tasting it for the last time" (119–20). As she had aimed to do at the beginning of her journal, Caro gets to the core of her existence. Like Avey Johnson, she has stripped away all her worldly baggage, preparing for a rebirth of her self; but unlike Avey, her rebirth will come with death. Impending death is the catalyst that makes Caro appreciate life and brings her to fruition.

Caro's final act of setting fire to Twin Elms may be seen as a moral gesture of resistance to its evil and her humiliating treatment there, a gesture asserting her humanness, courage, integrity, and self-completion. In cleansing the place, she also acts as a social critic, sounding the clarion against society's cruel treatment of the dependent elderly: Caro "transforms her death into an indictment of society's attitudes toward the aged and the infirm" (Bakerman 21). Dying as a social protester, Caro dismantles American culture's binary opposition between youth's activism and age's passivity.

An alternative may be to see in Caro's act despair, disintegration, and a retreat into numbness or madness, a gradual giving up of the will to love or care about life's beauties. It may represent a relinquishing even of hatred or of whatever connects a person to reality. Or her act may combine a little of both impulses, despair and affirmation, as Jane S. Bakerman suggests when she writes that "Caro burns down the home as a final act of despair *and* self-realization" (86; italics added).

Yet, regardless of how readers view the novel's conclusion, they cannot help but be overcome by its pathos, cannot help but feel catharsis at the holocaust of Twin Elms. Sarton has shocked readers into an awareness of some institutions' physical and psychological brutalization of dependent elders. It becomes difficult to countenance inhumane treatment of the ageless human beings that Sarton has brought to life through the journal writings of Caro. Sarton's *Reifungsroman* also increases our understanding of individual elders' thought processes as they begin to break down, the fears, the vulnerability, the intermittent befuddlement, the extra clinging to kind people as reality recedes, the torrent of intense feelings that sweep over them. Finally, Sarton's *Reifungsroman* shows us how an outraged elder challenges the association of old age with giving up by fighting dependence, indignity, apathy, and nonentity. Marlene Springer has said that Sarton is "one of the few writers to treat the aged, and particularly older women, with dignity without ignoring the threats of senility, the helplessness of physical decay, the frustrations of waning power" (46). Certainly she has accomplished these things in her portrayal of the heroine of *As We Are Now*. Caro Spencer is, in the Reverend Thornhill's estimation, a great human being. And most readers will agree with him, leaving the novel filled with admiration for Caro, despite the indignities she has suffered at Twin Elms.

HAGAR SHIPLEY: FROM PROPRIETY AND PRIDE TO WARMTH AND WISDOM

American literary scholars are discovering what Canadians have known for some time: the stature of writer Margaret Laurence. Laurence, who died in 1987, began writing novels in 1960 and was honored in 1972 by being made a Companion of the Order of Canada. She is known especially for her "Manawaka Quintet," a saga of the people of a fictional town in the Canadian prairies. *The Stone Angel* (1964), the first novel of the quintet, depicts the life of 90-year-old Hagar Shipley, a character in many respects similar to Caro Spencer. Strong-minded and independent like Caro, Hagar fights the horrors of institutional life, resists being incarcerated in Silverthreads nursing home by her son Marvin and daughter-in-law Doris. She sees Silverthreads as a direct route to stultification, insanity, and death: "Can they force me? . . . Make a madwoman of me. . . . Is it a mausoleum, and I, the Egyptian, mummified with pillows and my own flesh, through some oversight embalmed alive?" (84). She resists by running away from home, a flight not only to freedom and a reaffirmation of living, but also to self-knowledge and to the truth about her relationship with her other son. Instead of becoming mummified in her old age, she unwraps the layers of an emotional mummification that had throughout her life isolated her from the people important to her. This unwrapping—releasing and expressing Hagar's pent-up, petrified feelings—is the central movement of the novel.

Laurence's *Reifungsroman* is Hagar's first-person narrative. It consists of frequent flashbacks to important conversations of her personal history, a good deal of interior monologue, cathartic confessions of Hagar's past mistakes, and painstaking self-analysis. During Hagar's mental journey, she reassesses her relationships with her father, Jason Currie, her brothers Matt and Dan, her husband, Bram Shipley, and her sons Marvin and John. Like Jane Somers, she ruefully acknowledges her coldness as a young woman toward the men in her life; in old age she thaws enough to feel the passion and tenderness for them that she had hidden as a sign of weakness. Laurence's aligning of youth with coldness and age with passion unsettles our usual polarized ideas about the emotions of youth and age. Nonagenarian Hagar takes her place alongside other passionate elders like Jane Somers, Caro Spencer, and Mrs. Palfrey after recognizing how her pride and deference to propriety had petrified her capacity for joy and love. The stone angel is able to "melt with ruth" and reach out in love to her son Marvin. Experiencing love, fully humanized in old age, she can ripen toward death in a fruitful way.

The Stone Angel begins with a quotation from the Dylan Thomas poem, "Do Not Go Gentle Into That Good Night," which Caro also quotes from in her journal. Thomas's line, "Rage, rage against the dying of the light," could be the shibboleth of the dependent old; as they face the diminution of their powers and death, these elderly protagonists of *Reifungsromane* generally feel rage and are motivated by it. Maudie Fowler, Marcia Ivory, and Caro feel deep anger stemming from their forced dependency, or in Marcia's case, from the threat to her autonomy by social workers and coworkers. In the opening four chapters of Laurence's novel, Hagar Shipley rages against the dying of her life's light, against her failing health and increasing dependency on Marvin and his wife. Hagar's rage instigates major confrontations with her family. Although old age intensifies this rage, anger has always been a part of Hagar; it is at the very core of her personality, heritage, and Scots Presbyterian upbringing, linked to her pride, and epitomized in the family motto her father always quoted to her, "Gainsay who dare" (New 209). Patricia Morley has observed that besides this link between Hagar's rage and pride, Hagar's rage is also connected with "her stubborn love of life, her courage, her fighting spirit," but that despite this admirable spiritedness, her rage offends others, alienating them from her (Morley 85). This alienating effect of anger appears frequently in elders of *Reifungsromane*; Marcia Ivory and Maudie Fowler especially become repugnant to other characters because of their rage.

If Laurence had portrayed this raging behavior from outside Hagar's consciousness, readers would have been repelled by the abrasiveness, selfishness, and negativism of a crotchety old woman. They would have sympathized with the long-suffering daughter-in-law and son, who undermine their own health (they are in their 60's and Doris has a heart condition) while taking care of Hagar. Instead, Laurence places readers inside Hagar's consciousness so that they can experience Hagar's frustration at being dependent on Doris and Doris's irritating intrusiveness when she fusses around Hagar, poking and prodding to settle her comfortably. Readers understand Hagar's anxious attempts to read the glances and gestures exchanged between husband and wife concerning Hagar's lapses in memory, her incontinence, the issue of the nursing home, the results of her x-ray tests. In addition, using a common event of *Reifungsromane*, the fall, Laurence shows readers not just that it is difficult for Doris to lift up Hagar's considerable bulk, but also that it is mortifying to Hagar to be so helpless, as it is to Laura Palfrey and Caro Spencer. Similarly, readers see how it galls Hagar to reverse roles with her children: to be told that she wets the bed nightly, adding to Doris's laundry work; to be corrected when her memory fails; to be reminded that she cannot be left alone and that her children must hire a "sitter" if they want to go out to a movie. Hagar is caught between "fury and remorse" in her dependency on her children (59), sorry for being a burden to them, angry at herself for having to depend on them, and fully aware that she is incapable of managing her house by herself ("Everything is too complicated, the electric kitchen, the phone, the details to remember" 107). The first-person limited omniscient narrative and interior monologue enable readers to experience Hagar's frustrations, vulnerability, and, as Barbara Hehner has observed, Hagar's isolation from all the younger people around her (Hehner 42).

Thus readers can sympathize with the ragings of this frail old woman while also witnessing the burdens of her young-old caretakers. By urging readers to see both perspectives, as, for example, through Hagar's interior monologues and Doris's dialogue with her, Laurence is weakening the binary opposition between younger and older and encouraging mutual tolerance. These dual perspectives help Laurence to fulfill her commitment to an intense realism of characterization in which readers experience vicariously a character's life. She describes her own vicarious experiencing of her characters' lives in an essay surveying her writing career, "Ten Years' Sentences": "I have become more involved with novels of character and with trying to feel how it would be to be that particular person" ("Ten" 16). Readers of *The Stone Angel* identify with Hagar because the interior monologues compel them to imaginative sympathy for her. Laurence's use of the first-person narrative also enables readers to observe more aspects of Hagar's personality than she is aware of, creating irony in her utterances and exposing her unwitting self-deceptions (Lenox 27), as well as indicating how much she is learning about herself as she reminisces. Laurence explains her choice of the first-person narrative in *The Stone Angel*: "A first-person narrative can be limiting, . . . but in this case it provided an opportunity to reveal to the reader more of Hagar than she knew herself, as her judgments about everything are so plainly and strongly biased" ("Gadgetry" 56).

Despite the fact that first-person narratives often create sympathy for the narrator, readers may unsympathetically observe that Hagar bears her frustrating situation without much grace by harping on Doris for her officiousness, martyred posing, and bad taste in clothing. Although her petty criticisms of Doris may alienate readers, it must be understood that she really is berating Doris for taking care of her. She resents having to be helped to dress and undress, is mortified by having to "de-mummify" herself, exposing her aged body to Doris: "How it irks me to have to take her hand, allow her to pull my dress over my head, undo my corsets . . . and have her see my blue-veined swollen flesh and the hairy triangle that still proclaims with lunatic insistence a non-existent womanhood" (67). Putting herself under Doris's care diminishes Hagar's self-esteem and womanliness even more than the aging process undermines her sense of her sexuality (note also how Laurence writes the old woman's body here). In Doris's hands, she feels like a helpless child. Hagar also comments on the dehumanizing lack of privacy for the old, similar to that of the very young. *Reifungsromane* frequently compare the social positions of the very young and very old; Laura Palfrey and Maudie Fowler would agree with Hagar's observation about the two: "Sometimes very young children can look at the old, and a look passes between them, conspiratorial, sly and knowing. It's because neither are human to the middling ones, those in their prime" (4). By exploring Hagar's anger at her diminished status, her childlike dependency, and desire for privacy and respect, that is, by emphasizing her humanity without idealizing her, Laurence implicitly criticizes middle-aged society's insensitivity and disregard for dependent elders' damaged self-esteem, their shame and rage, their humanity.

Hagar further vents her anger at being dependent by aggravating the old wound she had inflicted on Marvin when she conferred favored status on his brother John. She attempts to chastise Marvin by declaring that if John were alive, he would not " 'consign his mother to the poorhouse' [Silverthreads]" (65). Besides such guilt-provoking manipulations of Marvin's self-esteem, Hagar offers words whose tone is at once reproachful, apologetic, self-pitying, and self-loathing, " 'I always swore I'd never be a burden—' " (31). The word *burden* suggests the stigma of dependency and bears the intensity of Hagar's shame at being dependent; it also reflects her anger at her children's view of her condition. Her interior monologue explains why Hagar violently lashes out against those who would make her leave her home and enter an institution; such a move would threaten her identity: "The house is mine. . . . My shreds and remnants of years are scattered through it visibly. . . . If I am not somehow contained in them and in this house . . . then I do not know where I am to be found at all" (31). Hagar is fighting to keep her world from shrinking materially, from mummifying, so that she can preserve her individuality and self-respect.

That Silverthreads, which would radically shrink Hagar's material and psychic world, threatens to suppress her identity is apparent in the imagery she uses to describe her reaction to the newspaper advertisement for the nursing home: "I am held, fixed and fluttering, like an earthworm impaled by children on the ferociously unsharp hook of a safety pin" (47). The phallic/rape image suggests that her children are patriarchal figures that would violate and destroy Hagar, and then classify her as a specimen of passive female senescence. However, she refuses to be classed with other elderly women as "unanimous old ewes," to be part of "the hearth crowd" that the matron of Silverthreads glibly generalizes about as they tour the nursing home: " 'Our old people just love to gather here, around the fireplace . . . older people don't care for picture windows. . . . They like the more traditional. So we had these [leaded windows] put in' " (85–86). Even though she is 90, Hagar is not ready to accept the stereotypes of senescence reinforced by nursing homes, to sit by the hearth, a nonentity without individual preferences, tastes, and thoughts. She voices her opinions and eccentricities vociferously, does not try to be the discreet soul of tact: "I do not have . . . [Marvin's] urge to keep the peace. . . . Tact comes the hardest of all to me now" (32). Old age offers this license for candor to Hagar and many other salty old heroines of *Reifungsromane*, like Caro and Maudie Fowler. Candor is a way of preserving individuality and developing personal authenticity.

In addition to exploring her anger and expressing her individuality, Hagar uses reminiscences to seek a more integrated sense of herself and to understand why her relationships with her men were unhappy, why her joy in living was so circumscribed. She thinks about "the prime matters" still unsettled, and, like Caro, works hard to settle them, to reach the core of her life and resolve her conflicts (81). Her reason for leaving home and journeying to Shadow Point—appropriately named because there she faces the shadow of son John in her past and prepares for her journey to the shadowy destination of death—is not merely to avoid moving to the nursing home, but also to unwrap her mummified feelings about her life: "Perhaps I've come here not to hide but to seek. If I sit quietly, willing my heart to cross over, will it obey?" (171). Finally, through the kindness and candor of a stranger, Hagar's heart does cross over. She extends sympathy to the stranger and, after he helps her to gain perspective on her feelings for John over a lifetime, she can finally sympathize with Marvin. Her reminiscences and experiences at Shadow Point enable Hagar to face her own "posturing and rationalization," to become one of Laurence's "self-honest women" (Blodgett 8).

Through flashbacks about her father, her brothers, Bram, and her sons, interwoven with Hagar's account of her present circumstances with Marvin and Doris, her x-ray tests, Silverthreads, and her journey to Shadow Point, readers become knowledgeable about Hagar's interactions with her men: the things said and unsaid between them, all those missed opportunities to express her affection despite the harsh words she did utter. Whereas Caro's reminiscences shore up her self-esteem and bring her momentary contentment, Hagar's reminiscences unsettle her, make her question her past conduct, and break down her alienating pride.

As Hagar's memories resurface, readers are transported to the youth of Hagar Currie and are able, despite the ravages of age, to see the same young woman that Hagar sees in the familiar mirror of the *Reifungsroman*: "When I look in the mirror and beyond the changing shell that houses me, I see the eyes of Hagar Currie, the same dark eyes as when I first began to remember and to notice myself. . . . The eyes change least of all" (33). Because readers can see the young woman within the old woman's shell, they learn about young Hagar Currie's soul at the same time that they learn what Hagar is discovering about the events and people of her life that have changed her into 90-year-old Hagar. In another mirror scene, Hagar, like Caro and Jane Somers, is startled to observe the signs of aging in her face while her mind's eye pictures young Hagar:

> I . . . see a puffed face purpled with veins as though someone had scribbled over the skin with an indelible pencil. . . . Below the eyes the shadows bloom as though two soft black petals had been stuck there. The hair which should by rights be black [the black of the youthful Hagar] is yellowed white, like damask stored too long in a damp basement (68–69).

The two poles of the young Hagar and the old merge in her mind until the mirror intervenes, offering grotesquely swollen, discolored images of physical old age; but psychically, the young Hagar and the old are not poles apart. Through the self-reflexiveness of mirrors and reminiscences, Hagar gradually begins to understand the psychic dimension of the age continuum: how she was molded in her youth and how she hardened and shrank over the years, ultimately turning into the old stone angel—or mummy—who became distant from others because she had "cared too long" about the opinion of the world (4).

In the opening pages of *The Stone Angel*, Hagar muses about Regina Weese Currie, the mother she never knew, through recalling her father's and others' descriptions of her. From these musings, readers see the roots of her polarized thinking about strength (male potency) versus weakness (female passivity). Hagar establishes an antithesis between her and her mother, Regina's "feeble ghost" being replaced by her "stubborn one" (1). She thinks with disdain of her mother's weakness in devotedly caring for Hagar's crusty old grandmother: "She [Regina] was a flimsy, gutless creature, bland as egg custard, caring with martyred devotion for an ungrateful fox-voiced mother" (2). The irony of these lines is apparent when readers consider Hagar's personality and situation with Doris and Marvin. Yet Hagar disparages Regina for her lack of fortitude, her passive sexlessness, calling her the "brood mare who lay beneath [the ground] because she'd proved no match for his [Jason Currie's] stud" (37). She is repelled at the weakness of "that docile woman," in contrast to her own "awful strength" (51), which she believes she has inherited from her stern Scots father.

Hagar's two brothers are said to take after their mother in tenderness and unspiritedness. She, in contrast, persistently struggles against any loving impulses, resists becoming a tender angel in the house (Blodgett 8). One reminiscence in particular shows readers this struggle against a gentleness inherent in her. Her brother Dan in a deathbed delirium is calling for their dead mother, and brother Matt asks Hagar to don their mother's shawl and comfort Dan. She is conflicted, wanting to sympathize and yet disdainful of Dan's weakness. Motivated by her pride in her own strength and a desire to dissociate herself from her weak mother, she is unable to do the tender thing: " 'I can't. I'm not a bit like her' . . . all I could think of was that meek woman I'd never seen, . . . I was crying, shaken by torments . . . wanting above all else to do the thing [Matt] asked, but unable to do it, unable to bend enough" (21). Matt winds up enacting their mother. Readers see Hagar Currie struggling to root out this sympathetic tenderness, see Hagar's pride preventing her from softening, a pattern that continues to harden her through her life. As Hagar remembers this experience, she recognizes it as a missed opportunity to reach out and perform an act of love for a brother.

From an early age, Hagar is uncomfortable when love is displayed, as her recollection of a scene with her father reveals. Their interaction begins in anger, Hagar's more comfortable state of feeling. Jason strikes her with a ruler to punish her for embarrassing him in his store. She is enraged at what she feels is the injustice of her punishment, but out of anger and pride refuses to shed a tear; readers witness the hardening process at work again. Awed by Hagar's strength, Jason embraces his daughter, his love supplanting his anger. Hagar describes her reaction: "He held me so tightly I was almost smothered against the thick moth-ball-smelling roughness of his clothes. I felt caged and panicky and wanted to push him away, but didn't dare" (7). In this recollection, Hagar reexperiences love as a claustrophobic closeness that made her want to flee. She would prefer to remember her father as a harsh, judgmental man rather than as a man even momentarily overcome by intense love.

In her old age, Hagar unwraps and acknowledges the loving side of her father, which she had swathed beneath the anger of two other confrontations with him in young adulthood. She also reassesses the consequences of her anger. Both confrontations entailed her efforts to leave her father, one by taking a teaching job after college and the other by marrying "common as dirt" Bram Shipley without Jason's consent. Jason won the first confrontation and Hagar the second. Yet her victory was a Pyrrhic one, in retrospect, cutting her off from her brother's and father's love and suppressing her love for her father. When he died, she was "too angry . . . either to mourn for him or want the stuff from his house" (55). Again the dry-eyed Hagar, out of anger and pride, edged closer toward the petrification of the stone angel. No psychic reconciliation with her father comes of old Hagar's reminiscing, but she is less convinced of the validity of her anger, more aware of its corrosiveness.

Memories also crowd Hagar's mind as she tries to make sense of her marriage with Bram. This review of her marriage conforms to the pattern found in most *Reifungsromane* about married or widowed heroines. Hagar's memories of Bram unravel and expose Hagar's feelings while in the present she is having her stomach x-rayed; she makes the analogy between the two processes: "I feel I must be naked, exposed to the core of my head. . . . And now I remember. I'm getting my stomach scrutinized, not my heart or soul" (102). Through the recollections Hagar does, indeed, also scrutinize her heart and soul. Readers learn with Hagar that she married Bram to defy her father, and symbolically, as Angelika Maeser observes, to oppose "the Father in a collective value-system [the Protestant patriarchal religious and secular ethos]" (153). Bram was an unacceptable husband because he was lower class, uneducated, and defiantly uncouth, hugging "surliness like a winter coat around him" (61)—as rebellious as Hagar, but as opposed to propriety as she is obsessed with it. Recalling these facts now, she finally understands that this is why they married: "We'd each married for those qualities we later found we couldn't bear, he for my manners and speech, I for his flouting of them" (69). When he flouted the proprieties, cursing or speaking rudely to one of her friends, the young Hagar always condemned Bram. The old Hagar revisits her judgments and reassesses her tendency to blame Bram: "It was so clear to me then who was in the wrong. Now I'm no longer certain" (61). A lifetime's perspective allows Hagar to see Bram's side of the issue and to realize that her discontent was shared by him: she always wanted him to behave so as not to disgrace himself and her, and he always wanted her to be a little less respectable (102). Neither could ever change the other. George Woodcock has pointed out that their marriage, which reflected "the Canadian condition," was doomed to clash: "The rigidities of invading mercantilism [were] opposed to the vanishing liberties of the frontier" (55); the Currie mercantilism clashes with the Shipley primitivism and libertarianism.

Through her self-scrutinizing recollections of Bram, Hagar also acknowledges for the first time that she married Bram because she was sexually attracted to him. Remembrances of sex past, a common element of *Reifungsromane*, haunt the elderly Hagar, as they did Caro, Avey Johnson, Kate Brown, Jane Somers, and Felicia Lord. She recalls the dance where they met, when he impudently pressed his groin against her; although outraged and mortified, she danced with him yet again (40). Woodcock explains metaphorically Hagar's earthiness and Bram's as a motivating factor in her marrying Bram: "Earth in the sense of land is . . . important to her, and it is as much to live on his farm as to be ploughed sexually by him that she marries the socially impossible Bram Shipley" (57). Hagar confesses to herself and readers, as her petrifying pride prevented her from confessing to Bram, her passion for her husband: "It was not so very long after we wed, when first I felt my blood and vitals rise to meet his. He never knew. I never let him know. . . . I made certain that the trembling was all inner. . . . I prided myself upon keeping my pride intact, like some maidenhead" (70–71). The irony of acknowledging such feelings at this point of Hagar's life is that "now there is no one to speak to" (150). Regret is the pervasive tone of this reminiscence. Like Jane Somers, she regrets having missed the opportunity to speak her heart to her husband, to share and develop her feelings. Hagar, the emotional virgin, never gave in to her passion even as she "sucked [her] secret pleasure from [Bram's] skin," never even acknowledged with joy their first-born son as flesh of Bram's flesh. She simply let him think that his sexual hunger for her was part of his crudeness, "an affliction with him, something that set him apart, as his speech did, from educated people" (102); and she repressed her own sexual appetite to demonstrate her refinement. Reminiscence and reassessment enable her as an elder to acknowledge her coldness, her failings in her marriage with Bram, as Jane Somers did.

The cruelty of her behavior strikes Hagar now as she considers, with pain, that Bram had really loved her. He was the only person in her life who called her "Hagar," who acknowledged her individuality and loved her for herself: "And now I think he was the only person close to me who ever thought of me by my name, not daughter, nor sister, nor mother, nor even wife, but Hagar, always" (69). As she recognizes his affection, Hagar is haunted by the line, "*His banner over me was love.*" Her pain comes from remembering her shame at his love's earthiness and her failure to recognize its sincerity and depth: "Love, I fancied, must consist of words and deeds delicate as lavender sachets, not like the things he did sprawled on the high white bedstead. . . . His banner over me was only his own skin, and now I no longer know why it should have shamed me" (70). Hagar sees with new wisdom that she should not have felt shame at Bram's love, as her puritanical "higher" culture had dictated, and that love may be expressed in many ways, not just through the refined words and deeds of romantic novels. Through old Hagar's reminiscing, the rigid categories of Hagar's younger years—love versus physical passion, honesty versus propriety—are dissolving.

Hagar remembers just one tender moment in all their 24 years of marriage when she reached out to him: after his beloved horse ran out during a blizzard; she said, "awkwardly, 'I'm sorry about it, Bram. I know you were fond of him.' Bram looked up at me with such a look of surprise that it pains me still, in recalling" (77). Hagar's pain comes from recalling his look of surprise because it was so rare for him to experience an act of tenderness from her. Even when about to give birth to their first child, she recalls how she could not muster affectionate feelings toward him as he expressed the hope that the child would be a son: "In that moment when we might have touched our hands together, Bram and I, and wished each other well, the thought uppermost in my mind was— *the nerve of him*" (88–89). At 90, she regrets other missed opportunities to articulate how she cared for him. She was so much better at articulating her anger and disgust when she told him she was leaving him to raise her son John alone.

Recalling the years apart from Bram, Hagar describes missing him in the night, like Jane Somers, but returning to her increasingly stony self in the morning: "I'd waken, sometimes, out of a half sleep and turn to him and find he wasn't beside me, and then I'd be filled with such a bitter emptiness it seemed the whole of night must be within me" (141). Through this reminiscing process, Hagar finally recognizes and assumes responsibility for the emptiness of her life. She regrets not being able to apologize to Bram as he lay on his deathbed and mourns for the years wasted because feelings had not been shared: "At that moment I'd willingly have called him back from where he'd gone . . . [to apologize], not knowing who to fault for the way the years had turned" (162). Hagar finally stops blaming Bram for being himself and starts blaming herself for her coldness. In her old age, an emotionally freer and more honest Hagar fantasizes revealing her heart to Bram, appropriately while the doctor is x-raying her innards ("*Bram, listen—*" 102). However, even in her fantasy, which is interrupted by the completion of the x-raying, the sentence fragment suggests how hard it would have been for her to speak her heart fully.

There is irony in Hagar's recollections of her marriage and some angry regretful tears for her own blindness concerning her husband, "anger—not at anyone, at God, perhaps, for giving us eyes but almost never sight" (153). Nevertheless, she has reached the core of her marriage and uncovered some "heart's truths," putting her married years into perspective, finally understanding the significance of the love between her and Bram. Readers who witness the melting into turbulent feelings of this formerly stony 90-year-old woman see the dismantling of the bipolar notion that youth is emotional, tempestuous and age is serene, impassive.

During Hagar's journey to her past she also acquires understanding of her relationships with her sons. William H. New comments that "only . . . when she sees more clearly her relationship with her sons . . . does she come really to see her very self . . . and her role in life"; only then can she depart from that earlier severe role and take on the role of loving mother, briefly, toward Marvin (New 212). She remembers Marvin as a boy, too much like Bram in ungrammatical speech, sloppy table manners, and family name ("Just the sort of name the Shipleys would have. They were all Mabels and Gladyses, Vernons and Marvins, squat brown names, common as bottled beer," 27) for the snobbish Hagar to value him and own him as her son. She recalls how Marvin, a good boy who did his chores, would hang around the kitchen after announcing to her that he had finished his chores, until she would impatiently order him to leave. Hagar does not consider why Marvin stayed or why she has kept this memory of Marvin, but given Hagar's stern style, it is likely that he was waiting for words of praise and affection not forthcoming from his mother. Old Hagar's recollection suggests another missed opportunity to express something besides irritation toward her son.

This memory creates a pattern when juxtaposed to two other memories of Marvin, one when he left for war (World War I) and the other several years after he returned. In both instances, Hagar is compelled to remember missed opportunities for communication of warm feelings between her and her son. She recalls as he left for war how young and vulnerable he looked and how suddenly overcome with love for him she felt, yet how inhibited by the impropriety of expressing her love: "I wanted to beg him to look after himself, to be careful. . . . I wanted all at once to hold him tightly, plead with him, against all reason and reality, not to go. But I did not want to embarrass both of us, nor have him think I'd taken leave of my senses" (114). Hagar's concern with propriety so restrains her feelings that she fears expression of her love might be taken for madness. Hence she forfeits the opportunity to speak, hoping Marvin will do so. But Marvin is as inarticulate as she, and so "the moment eluded us both" (114). Readers repeatedly observe that her impulse is to show her love, but that propriety and pride stifle the impulse. Similarly, she recalls overhearing a conversation between Marvin and John about Marvin's experiences in the war, and she again recognizes the missed opportunity for interaction with Marvin: "I wanted to ask him, then, where he had walked in those days and what he had been forced to look upon. I wanted to tell him I'd sit quietly and listen. But I couldn't very well, not at that late date" (161). All of these missed opportunities add up to the emotional emptiness of Hagar's life and her passionate regret at age 90.

What good does recalling all these missed opportunities with Marvin do for Hagar besides fill her with regret? Is she merely "choked with it now, the incommunicable years, everything that happened and was spoken or not spoken" (265), or can her new knowledge change or help Hagar in her old age?

"Furiously remembering" and reanalyzing the missed opportunities to express feelings humanizes Hagar, unwraps the emotional mummy, enabling her to express her fears about dying, to say, " 'I'm frightened' " for "the first time in my life. . . . Shameful. Yet somehow it is a relief to speak it" (271). Even more important, remembering empowers her on her deathbed to articulate her love for Marvin, fulfilling the need she at last perceives in him. Responding to his apology for being cross with her over the years, she compares him once again to John, but this time she lets Marvin "win" the competition; Marvin extracts praise from the stone angel, like the biblical Jacob, who wrestled with the angel for a blessing: "Now it seems to me he is truly Jacob, gripping with all his strength, and bargaining. *I will not let thee go, except thou bless me.* And I see I am thus strangely cast, and perhaps have been so from the beginning, and can only release myself by releasing him. . . . 'You've not been cranky, Marvin. You've been good to me, always. A better son than John' " (272). While the usual binary opposition between youth and age suggests that the young learn and the old stagnate ("you can't teach an old dog new tricks"), Hagar at 90 upsets this stereotype, learning from her past mistakes with Bram and Marvin and applying that lesson to Marvin. Hagar is fortunate to be able to rectify the wrong she did her son by words of praise that have the weight of the deathbed behind them. Marvin believes her, and though she privately classifies the words as a lie in relation to her love for John, she realizes that the dead (John) do not need what the living (Marvin) crave. This lie, a benevolent act freely bestowed on Marvin, is "yet not a lie, for it was spoken at least and at last with what may perhaps be a kind of love" (274). It may not be the kind of love she had for John, but Hagar finally realizes that love has many guises and that this reconciling love frees her from the bondage of her isolating pride (Morley 79).

Laurence's depiction of Hagar as she resolves the conflicts between herself and Marvin suggests that old age may become a time of increased affection and a stage for dynamic change, as well as a time to compensate for missed chances to demonstrate love. Laurence indicates that the resolution of the conflict between Hagar and her son is satisfactory by Hagar's reaction to the words she overhears Marvin say to the nurse outside her hospital room. The nurse comments on Hagar's amazing constitution and strong heart, and Marvin replies, " 'She's a holy terror.' " His words and tone give Hagar pleasure: "I feel like it is more than I could now reasonably have expected out of life, for he has spoken with such anger and such tenderness" (272). Marvin has given meaning and closure to Hagar's life by balancing anger and tenderness in himself, reflecting Hagar's resolution of the conflict between those two emotions within herself.

Hagar's reminiscing about her relationship with John is more complex but almost as satisfying in its outcome, which is remarkable considering John has been dead for years. Most of her important recollections about her flight with him from Bram to respectability and her relationship with John after he enters manhood occur during her journey to Shadow Point, where she interacts with a middle-aged stranger named Murray F. Lees. Hagar, through her journey, bravely rebels against propriety for the elderly, who are supposed to be passive and obedient to their caretaker children (she imagines a store clerk at Shadow Point looking at her "as though I were an escaped convict or a child, someone not meant to be out alone" 131); and although she endangers her precarious health by undertaking this adventure, she feels rejuvenated by ignoring the usual strictures which youth places on the old. It is as if she is making a new beginning in the abandoned fish cannery at Shadow Point as she descends "into her shadow self" and like Avey Johnson, undergoes "a kind of *rite de passage* [that] ends with repentance, confession, and peace" (Morley 80). Hagar is more fortunate than Caro in the outcome of her life review and ripening process. Her *rite de passage* allows her to understand the nature of her interactions with John, to release her pent-up emotions toward him, and to put her emotional house in order.

Like Hagar, Lees also flees ("F.Lees") from a constricting reality by going to the cannery to drink wine. These two lonely souls have communion with each other, performing a kind of religious ritual as they drink Murray's wine and eat Hagar's soda biscuits. Each becomes confessor for the other, listening as the other revisits his or her flawed interactions with loved ones. While Hagar at first maintains a polite distance from Murray, seeing " 'no reason for people forgetting their manners . . . wherever they happen to find themselves' "—including an abandoned cannery beyond the pale of society—Murray sees " 'every reason' " for tossing out manners (199) and shows Hagar how absurd and inhibiting adherence to the proprieties can be. The impropriety of the reserved, fastidious Hagar swilling wine from a stranger's bottle, sharing intimacies about her life, and huddling next to him to keep warm at first perturbs her, but her second thought reflects the change in Hagar: "To be frank, now that I give it a second thought, it doesn't seem so dreadful. Things never look the same from the outside as they do from the inside" (222). Forgetting about the proprieties, Hagar can concentrate on sorting out and reexperiencing her deepest feelings for John, with Murray as her mediator.

Murray's conversation with Hagar about his evangelical family and the son he lost becomes the catalyst for Hagar's confrontation with her failures and misjudgments concerning John and with her loss of John. Reaching out in sympathy to Murray for his loss releases Hagar's repressed feelings about John. Also, as Murray recalls the way his mother always worried about everything, from others' opinions of what he did to how she smelled in summer, Hagar learns more about herself and her own mothering; her response to Murray's portrait of his mother is ironic, considering how she had conducted her own life: " 'Well, the poor thing,' I say, clicking my tongue. . . . 'Fancy spending your life worrying what people were thinking. She must have had a rather weak character' " (202). Hagar apparently recognizes a weakness of her own character as she listens to Murray talk about his mother.

As she hears about his mother's influence on Murray, Hagar surely speculates about how she affected John, attempting to pass on to him the pride in her Scots heritage conveyed by her father, raising him as the grandson Jason Currie might have been proud of. Where did she go wrong with John so that he became an unhappy, cynical man, aimless, hard-drinking, bitter toward her? Her narrative becomes increasingly confessional, which is typical of *Reifungsromane*, as she reminisces in a *mea culpa* way about conversations between herself and her son where John described the pressures she placed on him out of love and ambition for him. She also remembers how dominated she was by the fear that something disastrous would happen to him, knowing that she could not bear to lose him. Her fear burdened John and became a self-fulfilling prophecy. John's personality could not take these pressures. Hagar now realizes she failed to raise John to be a strong person. So blind were her ambitions for him that she failed to deal with the shortcomings of his character.

Memories of his manhood asserting itself in sexual encounters with women also resurface, and Hagar again registers her discomfort with them and her incapacity to discuss these relationships with John. John's sexuality reminded her of her own empty bed and her longing for Bram during those years of separation (141). Moreover, as critic Clara Thomas contends, the plentiful references to the pharaoh in the novel suggest the presence of incestuous sexuality in Hagar (156), erotic feelings for John that she had difficulty acknowledging and that hampered her interactions with her son. Now Hagar acknowledges her own inadequacies in this area of her son's sexuality.

Hagar's recollections allow her to confront the fact that as he grew older, John increasingly resembled his father in his speech, attitudes, and dealings with women, even though Hagar had tried to turn him against Bram. Hagar recalls a conversation on this subject in relation to Arlene, the woman John loves and whose love threatens Hagar with the end of her ambitions for her son: " 'You like her, then?' 'Are you kidding? I'd lay her if I got the chance, that's all.' 'You're talking just like your father,' I said. 'The same coarse way. I wish you wouldn't. You're not a bit like him.' 'That's where you're wrong,' John said" (155). Hagar now realizes that her efforts to drive a wedge between John and his father had backfired, resulting in John's loyalty to Bram and bitterness toward his mother.

Hagar also shares with Murray her recollections of plotting with Arlene's mother to prevent the couple's marriage. Even though at the time she and Arlene's mother considered the separation a sort of "mercy-killing" of the couple's love (Morley 86), Hagar's recollection and reassessment enable her to accept responsibility for the fact that these manipulations brought the events leading to the calamitous death she had always feared for her son. By attempting to separate Arlene from John for a year, Hagar robbed him of his chance at real happiness, although she remembers saying to him, " 'I want your happiness. ... You'll never know how much. I don't want you to make a mistake' " (211). Her misunderstanding of what would bring John happiness and her misguided concern for propriety in his conduct (" 'you have to avoid not only evil but the appearance of evil' " 212) summoned John's despair, drunkenness, and the daredevil accident that killed him and Arlene.

In talking with Murray Lees about the night John died, Hagar experiences anew the pain of missed opportunities: "I'd had so many things to say to him, so many things to put to rights. He hadn't waited to hear" (216). She realizes that these missed opportunities completed the hardening process in herself: "The night my son died I was transformed to stone and never wept at all" (216). By recounting the story now, Hagar is finally able to feel "bereaved, as though I'd lost someone only recently" (222) and to cry over her loss. Soon after shedding cleansing tears, Hagar throws up the wine Murray has given her, further releasing her pent-up feelings and purging herself—like Avey Johnson—of her past sins toward John. Senescence in Hagar is now associated with the swift, intensifying flow of emotions, not with the cessation of that flow customarily connected with elders on Golden Pond.

Laurence creates a realistic discourse of senescence by combining Hagar's wine-sickness with the stress of the Shadow Point experiences and the cancer in her stomach, then depicting Hagar's consequent mental confusion from the first-person narrator's perspective: Hagar blurs the past and the present and mistakes Murray for John. Instead of resulting in the negative consequences readers would normally expect, however, this confusion actually enables Hagar to grasp the missed opportunity of asking "John's" forgiveness. We see the scene entirely from Hagar's perspective: "I see, bending over me, a familiar face. . . . If there's a time to speak, it's surely now. 'I didn't really mean it, about not bringing her [Arlene] here. A person speaks in haste. I've always had a temper. . . . You could come here in the evenings . . . I'd not get in your way' " (220). With these words Hagar confesses and repents of her wrongdoing toward John and Arlene and seeks absolution; the kindness of a stranger provides it. Murray does for Hagar what she could not do for her brother Dan on his deathbed; he pretends he is John: " 'It's okay . . . I knew all the time you never meant it. Everything is all right' " (221). Murray's charade, working with Hagar's moment of befuddlement, brings Hagar the contentment of thinking she has "put things to rights" with John. This scene represents the discourse of aging at its most intense and most influential in creating sympathy across the generations.

Because she now understands her relationships with her sons, Hagar at 90 knows who she is, appreciates her uniqueness ("Stupid old baggage, who do you think you are? *Hagar*. There's no one like me in this world" 223), and understands how and why her life has assumed its peculiar shape. While, as Angelika Maeser observes, it is too late for Hagar to live her life over, she is able to "reshape it imaginatively by coming to a realization of the forces which conditioned and bound her" (Maeser 152). This imaginative reshaping of her life and identity colors the days remaining to her so that she can live passionately and fully in response to other people. The internal ferment, growth, and ripening of Hagar during her last days are a reproof of the bipolar thinking that associates age with mental and emotional deterioration, hardening, or emptiness.

In the denouement of *The Stone Angel*, readers accompany Hagar on one last physical and psychic journey: the journey to her death in the hospital. Although the journey has its grim aspects, it also results in the ripening and preparedness for death that Caro Spencer yearned for but could not fully achieve. As is typical in the rambling, floating, and recursive narrative structures of most *Reifungsromane*, Laurence's readers vicariously experience Hagar's slipping in and out of consciousness, floating from dreams to reverie, to flashbacks, to present reality. To describe her intermittent, conscious efforts to reconnect with reality, Hagar uses the analogy of a fish rising to the surface of the sea: "My mind surfaces. Up from the sea comes the fish. A little further—try. There" (271). Like Laura Palfrey, she cajoles herself to keep going, to maintain contact with this world. And, as she copes with the pain of cancer, she conveys her craving for the medication that briefly dulls the edges of pain and sends her back into oblivion by focusing obsessively on the needle and the sensation as she is injected: "Only urgency remains. The world is a needle" (274); and "the needle slips into me like a swimmer sliding silently into a lake" (270). Readers suffer with Hagar and feel her ribs "hot with pain" (269), feel her body growing weaker, so that she is able to get out of bed only with the greatest effort to fetch her roommate a bedpan (269). The emphasis in *Reifungsromane* on the physical body and illness is especially evident in this part of Hagar's tale as she writes the sick, frail old woman's body. She describes the pain finally taking over her body: "Pain swells and fills me. I'm distended with it, bloated and swollen like soft flesh held under by the sea" (274); through this imagery, pain and dying are equated with drowning, being repossessed by the sea, the source of all life. Readers also see Hagar watching her world psychically shrink around her, from a hospital ward to a smaller semiprivate room, to a cocoon "woven around with threads, held tightly" (273). Within this cocoon, she will metamorphose into the butterfly-soul flying heavenward (Morley 81), as her body enters that narrowest, most private room, the grave.

Despite these grim aspects of her hospital stay, Hagar hails death's approach, saying to one of the nurses, *"It's important. It's—quite an event"* (252). She makes this event a full ripening of her life, gives it satisfying closure by preceding it with three important acts.

First, as a way of synthesizing the many recollections winding through her narrative, she fully acknowledges her responsibility for bringing her men lifelong unhappiness, deploring the mechanisms within her that stifled their joy and hers:

> Every good joy I might have held, in my man or any child of mine or even the plain light of morning, . . . all were forced to a standstill by some brake of proper appearances—oh, proper to whom? When did I ever speak the heart's truth? Pride was my wilderness, and the demon that led me there was fear. I was . . . never free . . . and [my chains] . . . shackled all I touched. Oh, my two, my dead. Dead by your own hands or by mine? (261).

Pride and propriety in her youth prevented her from speaking and feeling with sincerity and intensity, which she does now as a passionate old woman who gives the lie to the alignment, shared by the cultures of Canada and the United States, of youth with passion and commitment and age with impassivity and apathy. Her impassioned admission of guilt and mourning for Bram and John on her deathbed are followed by her conciliatory words of maternal love and attachment to Marvin, her second act. Her third act is her affectionate gift to the next generation, Marvin's daughter Tina, of her own mother's sapphire ring, to which she had been very attached. By expressing her love for her granddaughter in this way, Hagar finally sanctions tenderness in herself and her mother, voicing her love for the mother she never knew and linking all three generations along the age continuum. This linkage also represents Hagar's reaffirmation of femaleness and reconciliation with her sex, which she had from her youth disdained as weak, identifying early with the strength she associated with her father and all other men.

Although expressing this maternal tenderness may be seen as a concession to a rather stereotypical femaleness, Hagar Shipley in other respects remains nonconformist to the end of her life. She displays fighting spirit as she defies a hospital order by getting out of bed at night to give her young roommate the bedpan, which is also an act of regenerative, maternal love that spans the generations. And she irreverently refuses on her deathbed to do "the done thing," to beg God for mercy: *"Bless me or not, Lord, just as You please, for I'll not beg"* (274). Humility has never been Hagar's strong suit; she cannot even muster humility before God. Finally, she proudly refuses help and grasps by herself—out of "free will"—the water glass that critics contend is the "cup of grace," or "means of renewal in . . . a spiritual wasteland" (Thomas 160; cf. New 214, Blewett 36). Her spiritual pride, the same that flashed from the eyes of Hagar Currie, is still apparent in this stubbornly independent last act of Hagar Shipley.

Surely George Woodcock is overstating his case, however, when he says of the ending, "We are what we are, Margaret Laurence seems to be suggesting, and the nature we have been given will shape our lives and remain with us to the end" (58). Although her stubborn pride and independence have shaped her life in many ways, old Hagar has changed. Her pride has been tempered by a recognition of her failures in family relationships and her independence has been softened by love. She speaks love to Marvin, Tina, and her roommate in the hospital, and she listens for Bram's affectionate calling of her name in the night. Moreover, she displays a new capacity for joy that transcends conventional notions of age, laughing with her roommate over the bedpan, hearing with satisfaction the love in Marvin's voice. Such courageous personality changes and the reaffirmation of love, joy, and life that they lead to are typical of all the *Reifungsromane* in this volume.

Hagar has succeeded, more completely than Caro Spencer, in ripening toward death in a fruitful way, confronting the shadowy corners of her life and flooding them with the light of love. Her life has been more richly lived and felt in very old age than it had been over the previous nine decades. We may be reminded here of nonagenarian Maudie Fowler's contention at the end of her life that the last period, spanning her friendship with Jane Somers, was "the best time of [her] life" (122); Hagar's narrative clarifies and corroborates the truth of Maudie's assertion. The antiquated dichotomy between youth's intensity, emotional abundance, and capacity for growth and age's blandness, paucity of feeling, and stagnation collapses before Maudie's tribute to senescence and before the intense, full living of ripe old Hagar Shipley.

Conclusion: The Aging Woman in Society, the *Reifungsroman*, and Literary Criticism's Role

The stories of Kate Brown, Jane Somers, Maudie Fowler, Felicia Lord, Janet Stone Halloran, Adams's Laura, Laura Palfrey, Letty Crowe, Marcia Ivory, Avey Johnson, Caro Spencer, and Hagar Shipley proclaim that the aging woman's place in society is not beside a cozy hearth in retirement from life's adventures and human passions, but on the open road of life's possibilities, where she experiences and expresses intense feelings with newfound candor and where she seeks new commitments, new relationships, and personal authenticity. These heroines of *Reifungsromane* challenge the Golden Pond myth of peaceful, mellow, boring old age. They explode the social norm that expects old women to banish Eros from their lives. They defy the outmoded social expectation of passive senescence by taking charge of their lives, making changes, and traveling—inward, backward, forward into fuller, more intense lives and richer, more philosophical deaths. By leading "young" lives in middle and old age, these fictional heroines undermine the conventional binary opposition between youth and age.

Moreover, although they might not apply the term to themselves, these heroines emerge as extraordinary feminists, rethinking their goals, rethinking their social roles, restructuring their lives to be less rigidly proper, less phallocentric, less logocentric, more adventuresome, even more playful. These literary elders teach younger friends and relatives who interact with them, as well as readers who become involved in their lives, that spiritedness, intensity, introspectiveness, anger, love, and a deepening enjoyment of life's pleasures are likely to be characteristics of older women.

The writers who created these aging heroines are also feminists, political and literary iconoclasts: in the first place, simply for offering middle-aged and old women as protagonists instead of innocent, lovely ingenues or breezy, talented young professional women, thus extending popular journalism's venture of including elders in their portrayals of contemporary life; in the second place, for making these fictional elders fascinating, passionate, and real in their complexity—neither cloyingly sweet and poignant, nor completely dotty, nor impossibly haglike; in the third place, for reaffirming these heroines' femaleness even in senescence and for reconceptualizing the place of sexuality in older women's lives; in the fourth place, for creating a discourse through which readers can experience what it is like to be a middle-aged or old woman; and finally, for turning a bipolar concept of youth and age into that of an age continuum and leading us toward an ageless utopia.

This new discourse of aging recreates middle and old age through interior monologue, personal confession, and excerpts from protagonists' private journals. It also offers concrete descriptions of the physical and emotional aspects of aging for women— from remembrances of sex past to crushes on younger men and relief at the waning attentions of construction workers to varicose veins and a fear of falling—with what French feminist Helene Cixous describes as women writers' "peculiarly female attentiveness to objects" (Jones 365). This female attentiveness to objects is evident in the following catalogue of significant objects from the seven novels analyzed in this book, and most of the objects themselves are associated with women in American, British, and Canadian society: hearths, mirrors yielding details of fading, spotting, or wrinkling complexions; hairstyles and hair colors; clothing, such as Caro's silk blouse, Avey Johnson's trampled-upon mink coat, Marcia Ivory's outlandish mélange of summer coat, sheepskin boots, and straw hat, Mrs. Palfrey's short fur cape—certain to create "a decisive first impression" at the Claremont (Taylor 4)—and Jane Somers's fashionable garments cleverly constructed to camouflage age; household items that help give one identity, such as Caro's little pillow, glass vase, and bronze turtle (Sarton, *As We Are Now* 7), Mrs. Palfrey's familiar bottles of pills and pot of marmalade (Taylor, 4–5), Hagar's needle-point fire bench, oak chair, and china cabinet from her husband's and father's homes (Laurence, *The Stone Angel* 31). The woman's traditional cultural (American, British, Canadian) perspective in these *Reifungsromane* is also evident in this new genre's focus on aging's relationship to the domestic environment and the details of household management, for which such diverse characters as Marcia Ivory and Kate Brown have a passion and which Caro and Mrs. Palfrey also note when they move to new, alien environments: "dust under the bureau and an old piece of Kleenex" at Twin Elms (Sarton 7) and the "worn but not threadbare" carpet at the Claremont (Taylor 3). Through the female perspective and concreteness of their language, these *Reifungsromane* hold up a mirror to the aging woman and emphasize the role of gender in her aging.

In addition, *Reifungsromane* about the aging woman create their vividness and intimacy with readers by generally favoring first-person or third-person limited omniscient narratives that float over and through the heroine's memories, often accumulating strings of complex sentences, blending the past with the present, breaking down barriers not only between time and space, but also between rationality and fantasy, feeling and logic, wellness and illness, sanity and senility. Barriers also dissolve, ultimately, between protagonist and reader, between youth and elder. This kind of narrative writes the elderly woman's body in its varying American, Canadian, and English cultural manifestations, from fragile bones to silvering hair, thickening waist, solid centeredness, and candor of demeanor. It also opens up the aging woman's mind and heart to the reader: the fear and isolation, yearnings for love, liberation from the sexual baggage imposed on younger women, passionate involvement with other people and ideas, and developing integrity. The innovative narrative structures of *Reifungsromane* about aging women effectively answer major French feminist critics' urgent "call for new representations of women's consciousness" in literature (Jones 374).

If we further consider women's writing through the lens of some prominent French feminist critics, *Reifungsromane* emerge as intensely female in language and feminist in politics. Helene Cixous, in her explosive essay, "The Laugh of the Medusa," describes the impulse of women's writing: not "to take possession in order to internalize or manipulate, but rather to dash through and fly"; "woman's gesture [is] flying in language and making it fly" and women writers "take pleasure in jumbling the order of space, in disorienting it . . . emptying structures, and turning propriety upside down" (887). Contemporary women writers' *Reifungsromane* exhibit jumbling of time, space, and conventional meanings of words; challenge the proprieties of *Bildungsromane*; and undermine binary oppositions between youth and age, logic and fantasy, senility and sanity. As Cixous declares, woman—and, we would add, especially woman writing the body and psyche of the aging female—has "punctured the system of couples and opposition" (887). Hence, in *Reifungsromane* readers of all ages can fly freely through the memories, thoughts, and feelings of these aging heroines. There are also insistent, flowing rhythms in much of this discourse, especially in those retrospective passages and glidings of the heroines' (narrators') consciousnesses in and out of the currents of present reality, fantasy, and memory, rhythms that draw readers beyond phallocentric logic into what critic Julia Kristeva calls " 'semiotic discourse': . . . gestural, rhythmic, prereferential language" (Kristeva in Jones 363). Through this language readers feel within themselves, beyond logic, the sensations of women aging.

The seven female writers on aging represented in this book thus empower readers with what Cixous sees as the woman's "gift of alterability, . . . the wonder of being several" (889), so that readers, regardless of their age, can vicariously experience Laura Palfrey's fall or Jane Somers's erotic feelings, altering themselves while traveling back and forth along the age continuum to become these fictional women. What Cixous describes as the act of the woman writing may also be applied to the reader reading under the spell of this new discourse of aging: "When I write, it's everything that we don't know we can be that is written out of me, without exclusions" (893). Who has not wondered what they will become as they age and actually become old, what promise in them will be fulfilled? This discourse enables both writers and readers to project and speculate about "that which they do not know they can be"—older and riper selves.

Use of this female discourse of aging, the *Reifungsroman*, has another political (feminist) consequence, which the French feminists can elucidate. Kristeva describes her concept of womanhood as a political attitude created by virtue of woman's social marginality (Moi 164–66), rather than as an absolute, biological sex: " 'woman' . . . represents . . . any resistance to conventional culture and language" (Jones 363). Cixous also notes women's marginal position or even exclusion from history and describes women writing as "seizing the occasion to speak . . . [making] a shattering entry into history, which has always been based *on her suppression*" (880). Among the most excluded, suppressed women have surely been the old women of many races, classes, and cultures; once their childbearing function is fulfilled, these women have customarily been viewed as marginal, or worse, disposable. For older women to make a shattering entry into history through this new literary genre marks a true watershed in both literary history and cultural history. We cannot underestimate the political power of *Reifungsromane* to effect change in younger people's attitudes toward the elderly, in individuals' attitudes toward their own aging, and in notions of appropriate social roles for elders. Cixous appreciates the sociopolitical power of the pen—particularly the pen that is not a phallic instrument: "Writing is precisely *the very possibility of change*, the space that can serve as a springboard for subversive thought, the precursory movement of a transformation of social and cultural structures" (879). The *Reifungsromane* created by the seven women fiction writers in this book, as well as by growing numbers of other writers, may well serve as precursors to some

major sociopolitical revolution exalting old age for women, sub-
verting traditional myths of senescence by presenting plausible
social and psychological frameworks for proud, intense, active old
women.

Literary critics who enter the discourse of aging come under its
spell, educe and analyze its powerful influences for change, and
become partners with this radical discourse in its attempts to
change attitudes toward older women and old age. How? By
asserting, as Robert Scholes would say, "*another* textual power
against that of the primary text" (40). My subjective written
response to Laura Palfrey's crush on Ludo or Hagar Shipley's
exasperation with Doris contributes to and is also influenced by
the rapidly expanding intertextuality of the discourse on aging
women, the "network of relations with other texts and institutional
practices" (Scholes 30). As the number and power of texts on aging
increase and as critical notice of this emerging genre widens,
critics' power to elicit and influence new texts on the subject will
increase, setting in motion a vital, flowing current for change.

As a literary critic, my task has been to herald a new presence
in literary history, to introduce readers to a groundbreaking literary
genre that celebrates aging. This genre is at once intimate, instructive, reorienting, and anger-provoking because it explores the
humanity of the old against the backdrop of several societies'
lingering tendency to treat elders as if they "belonged to another
species" (de Beauvoir 806). The *Reifungsroman* insists, above all,
on the humanity of the old. Thus, the *Reifungsroman* in its role as
an innovative force in literary history works with the *Reifungsroman* in its role as a radicalizing presence in the cultures of the
United States, Britain, and Canada. The greatest cultural contributions of this genre are nothing less than to redraw the contours of
the human species and to translate into a kind of universal espe-
ranto the language of the "foreign country" of old age. The literary
critic intensifies readers' experiences with these radical texts on
aging, thereby extending the texts' cultural contributions.
Reifungsromane and their critics, finally, enable readers to see
middle and old age as, in Simone de Beauvoir's words, "a period

of life . . . possessing its own balance and leaving a wide range of possibilities open to the individual" (806–7). At the heart of the *Reifungsroman*, and the critical discourse that attends it, is the intoxication of pursuing these possibilities through old age into the true ripening of the human spirit.

Bibliography

PRIMARY WORKS: THE FICTION OF AGING

Adams, Alice. *To See You Again*. New York: Penguin, 1982.

Laurence, Margaret. *The Stone Angel*. New York: Bantam, 1981.

Lessing, Doris. *The Summer Before the Dark*. New York: Bantam, 1973.

———. *The Diaries of Jane Somers*. New York: Random House, 1984.

Marshall, Paule. *Praisesong for the Widow*. New York: E. P. Dutton, 1984.

Pym, Barbara. *Quartet in Autumn*. New York: Harper & Row, 1977.

Sarton, May. *As We Are Now*. New York: W. W. Norton, 1973.

———. *Mrs. Stevens Hears the Mermaids Singing*. New York: W. W. Norton, 1975.

Taylor, Elizabeth. *Mrs. Palfrey at the Claremont*. New York: Dial Press, 1975.

SECONDARY SOURCES: BOOKS AND ARTICLES ON AGING

Abel, Elizabeth, Marianne Hirsch, and Elizabeth Langland. *The Voyage In: Fictions of Female Development*. Hanover, N.H.: University Press of New England, 1983.

Adams, Alice. "On Turning Fifty." *Vogue* 173 (December 1983): 230.

Amis, Kingsley. "How to Behave." Review of *Mrs. Palfrey at the Claremont*. *New Statesman* 82 (August 27, 1971): 275—76.

Avorn, Jerome L. "Medicine: The Life and Death of Oliver Shay." In *Our Aging Society: Paradox and Promise*, edited by Alan Pifer and Lydia Bronte, 283–97. New York: W. W. Norton, 1986.

Bakerman, Jane S. " 'Kinds of Love': Love and Friendship in Novels of May Sarton." *Critique: Studies in Modern Fiction* 20 (1978): 83–91.

Bart, Pauline. "Portnoy's Mother's Complaint: Depression in Middle Aged Women." *Response: The Jewish Woman/An Anthology* 18 (Summer 1973): 129–40.

Beauvoir, Simone de. *The Coming of Age.* Translated by Patrick O'Brien. New York: Warner Books, 1972.

Begley, Sharon. "The Myths of Middle Age." *Newsweek* 101 (February 14, 1983): 71–75.

Bird, Caroline. "Growing Up To Be a 'Salty Old Woman.' " *Ms.* 12 (August 1983): 102.

Blei, Norbert. "The Art of Alice Adams." Review of *To See You Again. Milwaukee Journal*, May 16, 1982; located in Review of the Arts [microform] Literature, 1981/82, 91: A12.

Blewett, David. "The Unity of the Manawaka Cycle." *Journal of Canadian Studies* 13 (Fall 1978): 31–39.

Blodgett, Harriet. "The Real Lives of Margaret Laurence's Women." *Critique* 23, no. 1 (1981): 5–17.

Brothers, Barbara. "Women Victimised by Fiction: Living and Loving in the Novels of Barbara Pym." In *Twentieth-Century Women Novelists*, edited by Thomas F. Staley, 61–80 Totowa, N.J.: Barnes and Noble, 1982.

Brown, Margery Finn. "Do You Mind Not Being Young?" *McCall's* 109 (June 1982): 62.

Buckley, Jerome Hamilton. *Season of Youth: The Bildungsroman from Dickens to Golding.* Cambridge: Harvard University Press, 1974.

Callahan, Daniel. "Health Care in the Aging Society: A Moral Dilemma." In *Our Aging Society*, edited by Alan Pifer and Lydia Bronte, 319–39. New York: W. W. Norton, 1986.

Cartland, Barbara. "Getting Older, Growing Younger." *Saturday Evening Post* 257 (January–February 1985): 62–63.

Chen, Janet. "Old Age: You Are What You Were." *McCall's* 103 (November 1975): 40.

Chodorow, Nancy. *The Reproduction of Mothering: Psychoanalysis and the Sociology of Gender.* Berkeley: University of California Press, 1978.

Christian, Barbara T. "Ritualistic Process and the Structure of Paule Marshall's *Praisesong for the Widow." Callaloo No. 18* 6 (Spring–Summer 1983): 74–84.

————. "Trajectories of Self-Definition: Placing Contemporary Afro-American Women's Fiction." In *Conjuring: Black Women, Fiction, and Literary Tradition*, edited by Marjorie Pryse and Hortense J. Spillers, 233–48. Bloomington: Indiana University Press, 1985.

Cixous, Helene. "The Laugh of the Medusa." *Signs* 1 (Summer 1976): 875–93.

Collier, Eugenia. "The Closing of the Circle: Movement from Division to Wholeness in Paule Marshall's Fiction." In *Black Women Writers*

1950–1980, edited by Mari Evans, 295–315. Garden City, N.Y.: Anchor/Doubleday, 1984.

Daiches, David, and Jon Stallworthy. Essay on D. H. Lawrence. In *Norton Anthology of English Literature*, vol. 2, 5th ed., 2107–10. New York: W. W. Norton, 1979.

Daniels, Jonathan. "I'm Old and I'm Glad of It." *Saturday Evening Post* 240 (February 25, 1967): 8.

Davis, Karen. "Paying the Health-Care Bills of an Aging Population." In *Our Aging Society*, edited by Alan Pifer and Lydia Bronte, 299–318. New York: W. W. Norton, 1986.

De Mott, Benjamin. "Stories of Change." Review of *To See You Again, New York Times Book Review*, April 11, 1982: 7.

Didion, Joan. "On Self-Respect." In *Slouching Toward Bethlehem*, 142–48. New York: Farrar, Straus and Giroux, 1961.

Donovan, Josephine. *The New Feminist Moral Vision*. New York: Frederick Ungar, 1985.

Draine, Betsy. *Substance Under Pressure: Artistic Coherence and Evolving Form in the Novels of Doris Lessing*. Madison: University of Wisconsin Press, 1983.

Dunne, John Gregory. "Halfway Home." *Saturday Evening Post* 240 (July 15, 1967): 21–22.

Eagleton, Terry. *Literary Theory: An Introduction*. Minneapolis: University of Minnesota Press, 1983.

Elshtain, Jean Bethke. "Feminist Discourse and Its Discontents: Language, Power, and Meaning." In *Feminist Theory: A Critique of Ideology*, edited by Nannerl D. Keohane, Michelle Z. Rosaldo, and Barbara C. Gelpi, 127–45. Chicago: University of Chicago Press, 1981.

Fischer, Lucy Rose. *Linked Lives: Adult Daughters and Their Mothers*. New York: Harper, 1986.

Garfield, Johanna. "The Case Against Telling Your Age." *McCall's* 109 (January 1982): 124.

Gelman, David. "Growing Old, Feeling Young." *Newsweek* 100 (November 1, 1982): 56–60.

Gilligan, Carol. *In a Different Voice: Psychological Theory and Women's Development*. Cambridge: Harvard University Press, 1982.

Graham, Robert J. "Cumbered with Much Serving: Barbara Pym's 'Excellent Women.' " *Mosaic* 17 (Spring 1984): 141–60.

Gray, Paul. "Balances." Review of *To See You Again. Time* 119 (April 19, 1982): 78–80.

Green, Robert Michael. Review of *To See You Again. Baltimore Sun*, April 4, 1982; located in Review of the Arts [microform] Literature, 1981/82, 80: A2.

Gumpert, Martin, M.D. Article on aging. *Reader's Digest* 59 (December 1951): 61–63; condensed from *New York Times Magazine,* July 8, 1951.

Hailey, Elizabeth Forsythe. "Alice Adams Mixing Entertainment and Insights." *Dallas Morning News,* May 2, 1982; located in Review of the Arts [microform] Literature, 1981–82, 91: A10–11.

Hapgood, Norman. "On Growing Old." *Atlantic Monthly* 92 (November 1903): 688–89.

"Happy Old Age." *Chamber's Edinburgh Journal* 79 (1902): 197–99.

Harrison, Clara Emily. "Another Plea for Old Age Homes." *The Cornhill Magazine* 121 (April 1920): 426–30.

Hehner, Barbara. "River of Now and Then: Margaret Laurence's Narratives." *Canadian Literature* 74 (Autumn 1977): 40–57.

Hendrin, Josephine. "Doris Lessing: The Phoenix 'Midst Her Fires." *Harper's* (June 1973): 82–86.

Heyn, Dalma. "Why Some Women Age Faster Than Others." *McCall's* 110 (November 1982): 117.

Hill, Gladwin. "Baby Boomer on Age Wave for the Elderly." *Wilmington Star News,* Sept. 14, 1988, sec. 1D; rept. from Maturity News Service.

Howe, Susanne. *Wilhelm Meister and His English Kinsmen.* New York: Columbia University Press, 1930.

"How to Get Old and Do It Right." *Esquire* 83 (April 1975): 73–87.

"How to Grow Old." *The Nation* 83 (November 1, 1906): 365.

Jefferson, Margo. "A Black Woman's Odyssey." Review of *Praisesong for the Widow. Nation* 236 (April 2, 1983): 403–4.

Jehlen, Myra. "Archimedes and the Paradox of Feminist Criticism." In *The 'Signs' Reader: Women, Gender, and Scholarship,* edited by Elizabeth Abel and Emily K. Abel, 69–95. Chicago: University of Chicago Press, 1983.

Jones, Ann Rosalind. "Writing the Body: Toward an Understanding of *l'Ecriture feminine.*" In *The New Feminist Criticism,* edited by Elaine Showalter, 361–77. New York: Pantheon, 1985.

Kaplan, Sydney Janet. "Passionate Portrayal of Things to Come: Doris Lessing's Recent Fiction." In *Twentieth-Century Women Novelists,* edited by Thomas F. Staley, 1–15. Totowa, N.J.: Barnes and Noble, 1982.

Kapp, Isa. "Out of the Swim with Barbara Pym." *American Scholar* 52 (Spring 1983): 237–42.

Kingsland, Mrs. Burton. "Being Happy in Old Age." *Ladies' Home Journal* 17 (March 1900): 10.

Klein, Kathleen Gregory. "Aging and Dying in the Novels of May Sarton." *Critique* 24, no. 3 (Spring 1983): 150–57.

Kramarae, Cheris, and Paula A. Treichler. *A Feminist Dictionary.* Boston: Pandora Press, Routledge and Kegan Paul, 1985.

Kristeva, Julia. "Women's Time." In *Feminist Theory: A Critique of Ideology*, edited by Nannerl O. Keohane, Michelle Z. Rosaldo, and Barbara C. Gelpi, 31–54. Chicago: University of Chicago Press, 1981; originally published as "Le Temps des femmes," *34/44: Cahiers de recherche de sciences des textes et documents* 5 (Winter 1979): 5–19.

Kuhn, Maggie. "Grass-Roots Gray Power." In *The Older Woman: Lavender Rose or Gray Panther?* edited by Marie Moschall Fuller and Cora Ann Martin, 223–27. Springfield, Ill.: Charles Thomas Publishers, 1980.

Laurence, Margaret. "Ten Years' Sentences." *Canadian Literature* 41 (Summer 1969): 10–16.

———. "Gadgetry or Growing: Form and Voice in the Novel." *Journal of Canadian Fiction* 27 (Summer 1980): 54–62.

Leclercq, Florence. *Elizabeth Taylor*. Boston: Twayne, 1985.

Lenox, John Watt. "Manawaka and Deptford: Place and Voice." *Journal of Canadian Studies* 13 (Fall 1978): 23–30.

Lentricchia, Frank. *Criticism and Social Change*. Chicago: University of Chicago Press, 1983.

Levin, Martin. Review of *Mrs. Palfrey at the Claremont*. *New York Times Book Review*, June 27, 1971: 18.

Lohr, Steve. "British Health Service Faces a Crisis in Funds and Delays." *New York Times*, August 7, 1988, sec. 1, 1+.

Loughman, Celeste. "Novels of Senescence: A New Naturalism." *Gerontologist* 17 (February 1977): 79–84.

Lynes, Russell. "A Cool Cheer for Middle Age." *Look* 31 (October 17, 1967): 45.

McCluskey, John, Jr. "And Called Every Generation Blessed: Theme, Setting, and Ritual in the Works of Paule Marshall." In *Black Women Writers 1950–1980*, edited by Mari Evans, 316–34. Garden City, N.Y.: Anchor/Doubleday, 1984.

MacDonald, Barbara, with Cynthia Rich. *Look Me in the Eye: Old Women, Aging and Ageism*. San Francisco: Spinster's Ink, 1983.

Maeser, Angelika. "Finding the Mother: The Individualization of Laurence's Heroines." *Journal of Canadian Fiction* 27 (Summer 1980): 151–66.

Maxwell, Florida Scott. Excerpt from *The Measure of My Days*. *Southern Exposure* 13 (May–June 1985): 19–20.

Mbiti, John S. *Introduction to African Religion*. London: Heinemann, 1975.

Moi, Toril. *Sexual/Textual Politics: Feminist Literary Theory*. London: Metheun, 1985.

Moore, Pam. "What We Expect and What It's Like: Problems of Old Age." *Psychology Today* 9 (August 1975): 29–30.

Moore, Patty. "Old Before Her Time." Interview by Katherine Barnett. *Ladies' Home Journal* 100 (August 1983): 46–51+.

Morley, Patricia. *Margaret Laurence*. Boston: Twayne, 1981.

Nardin, Jane. *Barbara Pym*. Boston: Twayne, 1985.

Neugarten, Bernice L., and Dail A. Neugarten. "Changing Meanings of Age in the Aging Society." In *Our Aging Society*, edited by Alan Pifer and Lydia Bronte, 33–51. New York: W. W. Norton, 1986.

"New Outlook for the Aged." *Time* 105 (June 2, 1975): 44–46.

New, William H. "Life and Time: Laurence's *The Stone Angel*." In *Articulating West: Essays on Purpose and Form in Modern Canadian Literature, 207–15. Toronto: New Press, 1972.

"Old But Far From Feeble." *The Economist* 306 (March 12, 1988): 30.

"Old Men." *Littell's Living Age* 192 (March 5, 1892): 628–33.

"Older, Stronger, Wiser: Southern Elders," *Southern Exposure* 13 (May–June 1985): 10–13.

"The Outlook Upon Life of Extreme Old Age." *The Spectator* 90 (April 11, 1903): 566–67.

Peirce, Neal R., and Peter C. Choharis. "The Elderly as a Political Force—26 Million Strong and Well Organized." *National Journal* 14 (September 11, 1982): 1559–62.

Pifer, Alan, and Lydia Bronte. "Introduction: Squaring the Pyramid." In *Our Aging Society*, edited by Pifer and Bronte, 3–13. New York: W. W. Norton, 1986.

Pratt, Annis. *Archetypal Patterns in Women's Fiction*. Bloomington: Indiana University Press, 1981.

Pratt, Annis, and L. S. Dembo. "Introduction." In *Doris Lessing: Critical Studies*, vii–xi. Madison: University of Wisconsin Press, 1974.

Priestley, J. B. "Growing Old." *New Statesman* 72 (July 29, 1966): 161.

Purves, Libby. "Where the Hormones, There Moan I." *Punch Weekly* 289 (November 27, 1985): 11–12.

Ringer, Agnes C. Review of *Mrs. Palfrey at the Claremont. Library Journal* 96 (June 1, 1971): 2349.

Rose, Ellen Cronan. "The Eriksonian Bildungsroman." *Hartford Studies in Literature* 7 (1975): 1–17.

Rosenblatt, Louise M. *Literature As Exploration*. London: Heinemann Educational Books, 1970.

Rosenthal, Lucy. Review of *Mrs. Palfrey at the Claremont. Saturday Review* 54 (July 31, 1971): 25.

Ross, Val. "The Coming Old Age Crisis." *Maclean's* 96 (January 17, 1983): 24–29.

Rossi, Alice S. "Sex and Gender in the Aging Society." In *Our Aging Society*, edited by Alan Pifer and Lydia Bronte, 111–39. New York: W. W. Norton, 1986.

Said, Edward. *The World, the Text, and the Critic*. Cambridge: Harvard University Press, 1983.

Sarton, May. *At Seventy: A Journal*. New York: W. W. Norton, 1984.

Scholes, Robert. *Textual Power: Literary Theory and the Teaching of English.* New Haven, Conn.: Yale University Press, 1985.

Segrest, Mab. Biographical piece on Barbara Deming. *Southern Exposure* 13 (May–June 1985): 72.

Sheldon, F. "De Senectute." *Atlantic Monthly* 54 (November 1894): 668–73.

Shelley, Dolores. "A Conversation with May Sarton." *Women and Literature* 7 (Spring 1979): 33–41.

Sibley, Agnes. *May Sarton.* New York: Twayne, 1972.

Siegel, Jacob S., and Cynthia M. Taeuber. "Demographic Dimensions of an Aging Population." In *Our Aging Society*, edited by Alan Pifer and Lydia Bronte, 79–110. New York: W. W. Norton, 1986.

Silverman, Phyllis R. *Widow-to-Widow.* New York: Springer Publishing Co., 1986.

Singleton, Mary Ann. *The City and the Veld: The Fiction of Doris Lessing.* Lewisburg: Bucknell, Penna. University Press, 1977.

Skerrett, Joseph T., Jr. "Paule Marshall and the Crisis of Middle Years: *The Chosen Place, the Timeless People.*" *Callaloo No. 18* 6 (Spring–Summer 1983): 68–73.

Sohngen, Mary. "The Experience of Old Age as Depicted in Contemporary Novels." *Gerontologist* 17 (February 1977): 70–78.

Spacks, Patricia Meyer. *The Female Imagination.* New York: Avon Books, 1975.

Spender, Dale. *Women of Ideas and What Men Have Done to Them.* London: Ark Paperbacks, 1982.

———. "Modern Feminist Theorists: Reinventing Rebellion." *Feminist Theorists—Three Centuries of Key Women Thinkers*, edited by Dale Spender, 366–80. New York: Pantheon Books, 1983.

Springer, Marlene. "As We Shall Be: May Sarton and Aging." *Frontiers* 5 (Fall 1980): 46–49.

Suleiman, Susan Rubin. "(Re)Writing the Body: The Politics and Poetics of Female Eroticism." In *The Female Body in Western Culture*, edited by Susan Rubin Suleiman, 7–29. Cambridge: Harvard University Press, 1986.

Theodoracopulos, Taki. "Your Time Is Up: At Thirty-Five Even Playboys Have to Act Their Age." *Esquire* 99 (May 1983): 135.

Thomas, Clara. "The Novels of Margaret Laurence." *Studies in the Novel* 4 (Summer 1972): 154–64.

Thorn, Phyllis L. "Stories of Middle Years and Fresh Beginnings." Review of *To See You Again. Seattle Times*, May 9, 1982; located in Review of the Arts [microform] Literature, 1981/82, 100: A4.

Treichler, Paula A. "Teaching Feminist Theory." In *Theory in the Classroom*, edited by Cary Nelson, 57–128. Urbana-Champain: University of Illinois Press, 1986.

Vance, Arthur T. "The Flying Years." *Woman's Home Companion* 31 (January 1904): 17.

Voak, Sally. "Firm But Fair." *She* (February 1986): 100–102.

Wheelock, Martha. "May Sarton: A Metaphor for My Life, My Work, and My Art." In *Between Women*, edited by Carole Ascher, Louise De Salvo, and Sara Ruddick, 413–30. Boston: Beacon, 1984.

"Woman and the Age Question." *Harper's Bazaar* 33 (June 30, 1900): 578–79.

Woodcock, George. "The Human Elements: Margaret Laurence's Fiction." In *The World of Canadian Writing*, 40–62. Vancouver: Douglas and McIntyre; Seattle: University of Washington Press, 1980.

Woodward, Kathleen. "May Sarton and Fictions of Old Age." In *Gender and Literary Voice*, edited by Janet Todd, 108–27. New York: Holmes and Meier, 1980.

Yeats, William Butler. "Sailing to Byzantium." *Norton Anthology of English Literature*, edited by David Daiches and Jon Stallworthy. vol. 2, 5th ed., 1951–52. New York: W. W. Norton, 1979.

"Youth vs. Age." *The Spectator* 80 (March 19, 1898): 402–3.

Index

ABOUT THE AUTHOR

BARBARA FREY WAXMAN is Associate Professor of English and Director of Graduate Studies on nineteenth-century British literature, contemporary literature, ethnic literature, and the feminist pedagogy in the teaching of literature at the University of North Carolina, Wilmington, and is the author of numerous publications.